I0616356

BOOK 1

THOTH'S MESSAGES TO HUMANITY

BOOK 1

THOTH'S MESSAGES TO HUMANITY

PAULA RABENIUS

THOTH PUBLISHER
FRISKT VÅGAT
SWEDEN

ISBN 978-91-983539-0-7 (Paperback)
Also available on Kindle

First printed in Swedish in 2012 as *Budskap från Thoth – till mänskligheten*

Translation to English: Rita Borenstein
Support with translation and publishing: Aaron Rose, USA

Other books in English by Paula Rabenius:
Thoth's Tools for Humanity

Thoth Publisher
Friskt Vågat
www.thoth.nu
www.finndinkraft.se
info@thoth.nu

Contents

Part 1

Thoth's Book for Humanity

About Thoth

Thoth was considered one of the most important gods in Egyptian mythology. He was often depicted as a man with the head of an ibis or a baboon. In one hand he often held a rod that symbolized power and influence. In the other he held an ankh, the key of life.

He has lived on Earth under many names and titles. According to Egyptian mythology, he had roles within many areas as an intermediary, scribe, and author in science, religion, philosophy, astronomy, mathematics, and more.

He was the God of wisdom, knowledge, and the moon, lord of the sacred words, and guardian of the divine order, rituals, and secret knowledge.

He is associated with time and the teachings involving numbers, and he is considered to be the one who invented the art of writing and to be the creator of the 365-day calendar.

When he speaks about himself, he only tells briefly about the past and prefers to talk about the tasks he has at hand, in this time. Thoth himself says, "I came to Earth very long ago, and I have only lived one earthly life as a human. This was in order to be able to operate in the form I do today—that is, to communicate and convey messages to humans through this physical body.

"However, for a very long time I have been on Earth in another form. I worked in Atlantis and I was also involved during the heydays of Lemuria. I left Atlantis when the soil there was no longer cultivable, and I went to what you call Egypt. There were twelve of us who left Atlantis to start new civilizations at different locations. Together we created an Energy Matrix consisting of twelve etheric pyramids that form a grid around the Earth. These pyramids consist of thirty-six unique frequencies (see Part 4).

"On January 3, 2012, I sent the body (Paula) to perform a very big and important task on Table Mountain in South Africa. What she did there was to start the clock of the Creation Matrix; the last cycle of time began and the vortex of the element earth was turned in the opposite direction. This event triggered a pulse in Mother Earth that now slowly has risen up through the planet. In that this cycle has been started, my teaching to mankind has shifted from being about purification and cleansing to conveying how you can find and open the twelve keys to higher knowledge."

About Paula

Thoth entered into my energy for the first time in June 2009 during a trance development course in Malmö, Sweden. This was the start of a very interesting and exciting journey. During my childhood I could see spirits, and I was always very afraid of the dark, especially in certain places. Later in life I realized that this was because I feel energies, not just of humans, but also the energies of the Earth.

My first encounter with a non-physical human was at the Easter of 1975, when I was only four years old and my family was on a ski trip to Sälen, Sweden. I dressed up as an Easter witch and was allowed to visit two houses located very close to the lodging house we stayed at. Before I had time to knock on the first door, I met a man that I got afraid of. As he approached me I wished him Happy Easter, even though I was scared. I remember that the man looked transparent, and when we met he floated straight through me, through my body. I was scared to death and hurried back to the lodging house. I cannot recall if I told anyone about my experience or if I already at that point understood that this was not something to talk openly about.

This fear followed me through life, and I always felt that encounters with the spirit world were unpleasant. The positive experiences with the spirit world I have had throughout life have been in the communications with my guides. I have had several different guides who have come and gone, depending on the current situation. One who has always followed me is called Conoy, an American Indian chief from the Sioux tribe. He is a tall, stately man who has been my father in a previous incarnation. When I was twelve years old, he told me that one day I would work in the trance state and allow a higher energy to communicate through me. I was terrified and chose to suppress this information.

In 1987 I went to New York on a preparatory course for High School studies. The visit to New York awoke something in me that I could not suppress. I was sixteen years old and had never been abroad, and of course I did not know New York. In those days Sweden had only two public TV channels, and I was not as urbane as the youth of today. When I arrived in the center of New York City for the very first time, I knew my way about. I could even notice changes that had occurred, and I found my way all over the city. I was of great help to the other young people who participated in the course.

At the age of eighteen, thanks to the events in New York, I went to my first meeting with a medium in Stockholm. The first words she said to me were, "You have recently been visiting New York City, and you knew your way about." She told me that I had lived there during my previous life, that my name was Sandy, and that I had lived in the Bronx. Concurrently with her continued description of that life, I saw inner images of it—of the family, the housing, and important events. In that life I died in a car accident, only eighteen years old. The year was 1956. I chose to go down into a new life and a new body very quickly, since I felt that that life was too short. One of my weaknesses had been that I had wanted to do everything, preferably at once. The medium informed me that in this present life I could take my time. This time I would get to experience the feeling of living my life to completion. After this meeting I attended several meetings, sessions, and séances of various kinds and of varying quality. I also began to read books on the subject.

In the year 1994 I met a woman who was a teacher of Reiki healing, and that became an opening to new insights for me. In the year 2000 I graduated as a Reiki master, and I began to work with healing, sessions, and massage. In the following years I took several courses in mediumship, animal communication, tarot reading, and a whole variety of other subjects. At that point my husband thought that I was practically throwing my money away, and he wondered after each course what it would lead to.

I avoided the subject of trance, because I still thought of it as something unpleasant, and I felt that I would never be able to allow a spirit to go so deep inside of me that I could not control the situation. With each course I became increasingly sensitive, and I found it very difficult to "disconnect" from the spirit world.

In the year 2001 I was faced with a "spiritual" burnout, and Conoy then told me that the only way for me to come back to live my life to the fullest was through meditation and learning how to "shut down." I then met a medium who taught me how to turn my contact with the spirit world off and on. Moreover, I started to meditate. I meditated daily, in the beginning for short moments, which later on became longer and longer. I got my energy back and have since then been meditating almost every day, both alone and in different groups.

In the year 2003 my family and I chose to move permanently to our summerhouse in Dalecarlia to live in a more peaceful surrounding. This resulted in me getting the peace I needed to develop my spirituality and sensitivity on a deeper plane. I met many like-minded people through meditation groups, and together with some friends, I formed a group that met regularly for drumming, meditating, healing, and communicating with the spirit world. It was with these friends I traveled to Malmö for my first meeting with Thoth, a meeting that led to the creation of this book. In December of 2011, Thoth declared that his words were to become a book, a book that would suit the modern human being and make her or him understand, without complicated old-fashioned language.

During the years of 2010–2012, all sessions with Thoth were recorded and transcribed, and thereby resulted in the following texts. I have chosen, as far as possible, to quote Thoth word for word. The texts are arranged and compiled in a way so that they fit into the context of the chapters in the book. When Thoth speaks to humans about "the keys," he almost always mentions them by saying, "We shall open the keys," a phrase that many people react to. How do you open a key? This saying probably has to do with encryption, in order to hide and to open information. The key in this case is an encrypted code. The code is opened, which is the same thing as the key being opened.

Introduction—Thoth's Own Words

The content of this book comes from me, Thoth, who in this time have come to Earth to inform you humans about a very old knowledge that has been forgotten and will now be brought to light again.

The Earth is located in the middle of the spiral in the middle of the Universe and close to the black hole. Time is going faster and the Earth is vibrating more swiftly.

I have come down to Earth to communicate with humans for many reasons. One is to be present with humans in the New Age, which I also call "the new Golden Age of Light." Things change daily around you on Earth. I have come to speak to you both individually and in groups, to help you set yourselves free from fears and blockages that prevent you from living in total harmony and balance. I want to help you find your own inner voice again, which you need in order to work with liberating yourselves from your blockages and traumas, from both previous incarnations and present lives. Experiences from past lives, whether they have been here on Earth or in other places, may need to be purified for a smoother transition into "the new Golden Age of Light." Therefore it is of paramount importance that "we," who come down to Earth to help the humans, reach out to as many as possible. We reach out to many more people than those who meet us in lectures and courses, because they affect their near and dear ones, who in turn affect others. This leads to an automatic spreading, like ripples on water.

You come from a non-material world, and you are descended into a material world. Now you have to learn to live in a material world in a non-material way. Start to sort out and work with that which is the meaning of your lives. None of you were born by coincidence. You have chosen your family, your situation, the people around you, and the relationships you have.

Sometimes you make less good choices, and the reason for this is often because you live the lives of others, you adapt yourselves to others and the society you live in. Everything you do—every word, every thought, every action—affects your close relationships, which in turn affect groups which further affect the society and the entire Universe. Everything that happens in the Universe is transformed down and affects the society, the group, and the single individual. You are all interconnected with each other like in a grid, like rings in rings. Do you now understand that everything affects everything?

There are many events in your lives right now that occur in your unconscious mind. This means that you are all actually unconsciously aware of the changes in frequency that have happened and are about to happen here on Earth. We move from the third dimension, or as I prefer to say, *the third density level*, further up into the fourth before the end of this year, and eventually up to completion in the fifth level. It means that all of you have agreed to join this journey already before you were born.

Many people may choose not to step up into the frequency of the fifth level. It is a free choice, and it's a matter of the level of development that you have achieved and the level of development that you want to continue to work at in your future incarnations here on Earth or in any other place in the Universe. Many people feel worse now than ever, and this is because their bodies have not yet been calibrated up to a higher frequency, and therefore they are not in tune with the vibration of Earth. I often speak about purification, how to manage to be as pure as possible in order to be able to absorb the new frequencies and adjust the body to the rising of the Earth's frequency that is ongoing right now. Humans will have the choice to follow, to be raised in frequency, or, so to speak, remain in the third density level. Not even I can prophesy what the future has in store and how it will unfold. My mission is to help as many as possible on the way.

One of my other missions is to help people not to go astray on side paths, but to stick to the main road. I awaken that which you have inside of you so that you yourselves can find your way back to your main road, the road you chose for this life. My job is not to tell you which road to walk, because then I would break the laws of the Universe.

You all make conscious choices in life, and you don't need to live in suffering. Who said that you are not going to bring positive experiences from this very life to the memory bank of your soul? Many people think that one has to suffer in order to learn and evolve. You create your own myths and tales, and you yourself choose how to utilize your experiences.

You ask questions like "Who am I?" and "What is my mission in life?" Now I want to ask the questions to you: "Who are you?" and "What is the meaning of your life?" I often tell people, "Look at yourself in the mirror every morning, deep into your eyes. You will get answers. One day you will see what a fantastic soul you are, and what strength you have and carry with you." Every one of you has chosen your life. You have a lot to learn.

I am also here on Earth now to inform man of the higher knowledge that was hidden from humans long ago. It was hidden for many reasons. One was their inability to control their egos. The egos grew stronger and stronger in the human bodies in a way that was not intended from the beginning. There was a belief that the higher knowledge could be incorporated with the earthly frequency level, but now we know that this is not possible. In order for the higher knowledge to not be abused again, Earth and consciousness must now be raised from the third density level to a higher frequency, and we all have to follow.

For a long time there have existed enlightened Masters on Earth. These are chosen individuals who have carried the higher knowledge from generation to generation. One cycle is now to end and a new one shall begin. I have been waiting for this for a very long time, to have the opportunity to open up.

All knowledge that has ever existed is about to rise to the surface. Not just the teachings of the Egyptian age, but the knowledge of all early eras that have existed during the Earth's existence are about to converge and create a unity. It is now time to turn the keys and bring forth this knowledge.

Every one of you carries the truth within you. Each of you was born with all this knowledge stored in your bodies; it only needs to be released and you will remember everything. This means that you actually don't need to meet me or others who mediate higher knowledge.

In these texts I give you the tools to find your inner keys to open the doors that lead to your inner true knowledge.

My most important message to mankind is about love for yourselves—to see yourselves as the fantastic individuals you are. Many of you have very strong social imprints that are difficult to let go of and free yourself from. If you are not freed from strong imprints, it will be difficult for you to face your emotions. It is your emotions and your emotional life that often create blockages. You get the wrong idea about who you really are, and this will follow you life after life. You don't consider yourselves being worthy; you put the blame and shame on yourselves. This creates anxiety and disease. You yourselves choose if you want to free yourselves from these blockages.

One reason for choosing to incarnate here on Earth as a human being is precisely that here one can live through different emotional stages; one can live out one's emotions and feel them fully, whether they are high or low in nature. But this thing with emotions has its good points and bad points, so to speak. Emotions affect you and your state of mind, so that you live via your mind, with the ego as director. Your ego can no longer control your life; it has to be mastered. It is time for the soul to become the director and to be in command. The goal is that you now shall live through your hearts and find yourself there. Then the room for the mind gets smaller and smaller. This is a difficult task for many humans, who have lived many incarnations in the same way. But you cannot free yourself if you don't have the courage to confront your obstacles.

This time is the time for the opening of your hearts. In order to live in a non-material consciousness, it is required that the heart is opened. Your subconscious and your inner higher knowledge will be reached if your heart is opened. How do you open your hearts? Start by affirming positive thoughts to yourself every morning.

Know that time, life is an illusion, a tale created by yourself. Time does not exist in my world. Linear time is something that humanity has created to make its existence more comprehensible. When I told you before that old knowledge is rising to the surface and that everything that has ever existed will become a unity, this also includes the aspect of time.

It is important, from this day on, to only live in the now and to let go of that which has been; it does not exist anymore. From today onwards you only move forward, day-by-day, by being in your heart. This means that you have to start letting go of your thoughts about material things around you. You also must try to give up the wandering about on side paths and try to get up on the main road, the road you yourselves have chosen to follow in this very life. You will gain in-depth understanding of this, and when you finally understand that time does not exist, but that everything happens here and now, you will automatically get answers to many questions that you carry within you.

For the years I have been in this body and met people, everything to date has been about purifying and cleansing your physical bodies. Now you can begin to work in earnest, on the level you are intended to do and will do—that is, to open up the collective consciousness again. This is going at a tremendous pace and keys are opening up for higher knowledge along the way. This gives access to all knowledge that has ever existed in all forms, in all civilizations, and on all planes. Realize that if you have trust and let go of your imprints, you have the opportunity to use the knowledge.

Your task is to change your thought patterns and go into the different frequencies of the twelve respective pyramids and start to work with them, either individually or in a group. Each pyramid contains a key to healing and curing, and you will get the answers to all you have ever wondered. At the same time, you will be transformed so that you can meet the New Age and the challenges that lie ahead. Your thoughts must start changing so that you can reach your highest potential.

When you start to work with the frequencies of the pyramids, you will notice that some are easy and others are more difficult to go into and enter upon. Always return to Pyramid number 1 to gather strength if you are having problems to continue. Of course, this depends on how close in frequency you are to the respective pyramid, your background, your lives, and the experiences you have brought with you on your path, both between and during different lives on Earth.

Part 2
Thoth's Explanation
of the Cosmic Plan

Earlier through the centuries, very *complicated* and difficult *explanatory models* were presented. This model is very simple, so simple that everyone should be able to understand their individual place in the Universe. Many prophets have conveyed this knowledge with incomprehensible words and difficult formulations. I hope that you will understand my words. This is a long process to explain and I will not go deeper into it, but by understanding the descending transformation and by getting an understanding of your background, you will get help on your way forward. It also helps you to make the right choices in life from today onwards.

Everything in the Universe is a process that started with a sound, a tone. Everything consists of this primordial sound that transmits an uninterrupted motion, that is, a frequency, which spreads like ripples on water, wider and wider. Even man consists of this primordial process.

Matter was gradually evolved out of a formless energy, an energy that from the beginning was without mass. In a wider perspective, one could say that everything consists of air, which gradually became denser to create matter. Thus, what happened was that a tone, a sound, arose and created the first seed for the origin of matter. This seed divided, and this started the great seed division, a process that led to a wider and wider division, which created more and more seeds. Out of these seeds an energy cloud was created, consisting of a great number of soul energies that were descended to different places of creation.

When I speak of your home, I speak of the particular place where your very first life in etheric form took place. Many people have a very strong homesickness for that place. You have lived many lives in many places in the Universe, not only in a human body, but your home and what you feel drawn to in your hearts is your place of origin. Everything in your physical bodies is identical to the creation of the Universe, or the Big Bang—that is, everything in the human body is an image of how the process of creation came about at the birth of the Universe.

At the same time as you were descended into physical form, an image of the creation process of the Universe was created in each individual. Macro cosmos and micro cosmos. There is a saying that you use: "As in Heaven, so on Earth." The cell is an image of what happens in the Universe, and the atoms and the molecules are images of the cell, and so on, all the way down to the smallest possible particle.

This beginning also started the evolutionary development for all planets in the entire Universe, including the planets circulating around your Sun, like the planet Gaia, your Earth. Accordingly, the tiny, original seed also created the planet Earth. The descending transformation to Earth took place step by step, and many souls have now walked through the Matrix that was built about 16,000 years ago. When you are descending, you are traveling down through different frequency layers. As a result of this, different personalities are also created; it is not just heredity from the genes of the mother and father that control the personality.

When you travel through the frequency layers you, among other things, pick up characteristics, depending on the position of the zodiac in the firmament. You encode tones of sound and light until you eventually come down to your galaxy, the one you call the Milky Way. There you are also affected by all the planetary systems that exist and their frequencies.

Finally you come down and enter into the Matrix (see Part 4). There you are transformed down into what we call the Atmic body, and further down, layer by layer, into the Metapersal body, until you come to the bodies that you recognize as the Causal, the Mental, the Astral, the Etheric, and finally the Physical body.

The bodies preceding the Physical body create an outer layer, which you call the aura. Your aura is connected to your chakra system, which consists of twelve chakras. There are seven chakras inside the body and five outside of it. In addition to these twelve chakras, there are also several smaller chakra areas. Everywhere in your physical bodies, energy pathways run that maintain the levels of energy to keep your physical body intact and healthy.

These energy pathways continue on in a larger perspective, to what I call the macro cosmos, and are also transformed straight down to Earth. The Earth has energy pathways, just like your physical bodies, and a chakra system, just like your energy bodies. These systems, of course, continue up in your Milky Way and further up in your Universe and the other twelve Universes and their twelve Universes. Do you see how everything is connected? You are all created like rings in a chain; you are all connected with each other. When you think a negative thought about your neighbor or someone around you, you think this negative thought about yourself at the same time. Everything in your lives starts by each person's thought.

You carry a lot of adaptation inside you, to be good, to be enough, and so on. A lot of people also gradually develop feelings of guilt, shame, anxiety, and worry. All the time you are walking around with a seed in your stomach saying that you long for home, that you don't fit in, wondering if life is not more than this, wondering what am I doing here, and so on. You don't need to long for home; you can at any time return home in a meditative state.

The most common questions I am asked by people I meet are "Which is my path to walk? What is the meaning of my life? What am I supposed to accomplish? My life must have a higher purpose?"

You all have a higher purpose. On the basis of this higher purpose you made a choice to go into a body and be born exactly here and now, with the parents and in the location that you have chosen yourselves. You have created your tale yourselves. It is only you yourselves that can change the tale to become what you once decided it to be. You yourselves choose all meetings in your lives and whether you are going to wander about on side paths or travel on the main road.

You chose a long time ago to start your incarnations on Earth to develop your energy, the energy which you in earthly speech call soul. This means that you constantly strive to reach a higher spiritual consciousness level. Some chose to incarnate on Earth when their own system decayed, so to speak. All of you have, of your own free will, chosen this incarnation and the walk to reach the All in the center of the Universe and the total balance, from where you never again need to return to physical form or work as guides. Everything is about peeling the onion layer by layer, in order for you to reach your interior and open the higher contact again and to travel through time and space whenever you like. You have chosen your lives yourselves; everything and everyone, your parents, your country, your location, and everything around you.

Changes in the New Age / The Transformation

Many things will change in the New Age—your way of communicating, eating, and dealing with disease, among other things. In the New Age, disease will not exist. You will not carry feelings like anxiety, guilt, shame, and abandonment. The way of dealing with disease will be different.

You will get all the answers you seek, and you will not need to go to an old man like me for information. All answers are within you, and your consciousness will be opened during the coming transformation. You will open up your own inner knowledge, the original knowledge from the beginning, and again learn to manage energy and to create by using tones, light, and crystals. You will receive new abilities that you right now are unaware of, and it is very good if you start opening up your senses, begin practicing and playing with energy, and work telepathically on a deeper level than before.

Also, healing work will be changed to another level than before. It is important that you first of all heal and purify yourselves and then help others around you. Of the children born in this era, many are pre-programmed to cope with the transition and the New Age. Many of the children feel bad because the frequency on Earth is too slow, compared to their original energy. It is important to have an understanding of these children and why they suffer so much right now. A lot of people in the world will need help to reach a higher level of consciousness. Maybe some of you will become the ones who guide them.

The structures and hierarchies of society are about to dissolve. Old knowledge, but also new technology within areas like energy supply and means of transport, will be revealed. Much of this will be given to humans in a meditative state. Be aware, and write down or draw everything that comes to you. The information may be given to you in symbols, words, pictures, and such simple forms as what you call curlicues. Even though you don't grasp what comes to you right away, it might be of use later on.

Food and Drink

Soon you will notice that your food intake has to change to less solid food. The food you eat should be purified and healed—for example, by you blessing your food and drink. You do this in the easiest way by using the thirty-six sacred frequencies of the twelve pyramids and the frequencies of the planets (see Part 4).

Put your hands on/around the food/drink and have the intention, the will, that the food will be filled with the thirty-six frequencies and that it will be charged with what you need at the present moment. You will then get everything you need, and your organs will be helped to vibrate in the right frequency/tone through what you eat and drink. No matter where the food has grown, it will be charged with the frequencies and become filled with energy. This is important, because Mother Earth cannot give you all the necessary frequencies, due to poisoning and acidified soil.

Trust that your body knows exactly what is no longer in harmony with your vibration. The body knows what is toxic to you in particular. You will no longer desire to eat what you previously did; the body cannot handle food with low frequency. Reduce the amount of food, but eat balanced (many different sorts of food). Cook your food with the intention that everyone who eats it will get what they need. Have focus and balance when you cook, be here and now, and give love to the food.

Time

Linear time is an illusion and was created on Earth just to make life more comprehensible. You will have a deeper understanding of this, and when you finally understand that time does not exist, but that everything occurs here and now, you will automatically get the answer to many questions that you carry inside.

It is important to let go of what has been, to be in the present moment, otherwise your intuition will be prevented from becoming clear when dealing with all the choices you are facing. Live here and now, as if every day is your first. Every morning is a new day. Look at time as three pieces of paper next to each other—one with what has been, one with what is now, and one with what is to come. Imagine that you now put these pieces of paper in a stack on top of each other, and you will then see that the three pieces still exist, but in a common place and at the same time. This means that even past and future exist now. It is only your consciousness that blocks your possibilities to be in all places simultaneously.

Homesickness

Why do so many find it difficult to accept and understand their choices in life? They are happy with their lives, but still they carry an inner torment of some kind. Their homesickness is so strong that they feel restlessness in their bodies, which they cannot associate with anything in their lives. They experience that they never feel really at home anywhere.

At this time, the Earth rotates to adjust itself towards the center of the Universe. We have been there before; this is nothing new. But the changes that happen with this rotation alter the Earth's atmosphere and magnetism, and this affect the frequencies here on Earth. This affects all of you physically, psychologically, emotionally, and spiritually.

When you have difficulty finding inner stillness and peace, it is time for you to initiate a process of change and start to communicate inwardly. It is time to find your own power and turn inward for answers. Try to focus on your interior. You will find feelings like sadness, joy, loneliness, and abandonment, and you will discover events, situations, and abusive treatment that you have felt and met during all your incarnations, even those from your future, which you now know exist parallel to the present time. Start by understanding that you have made conscious choices. Even though you feel that the body is a physical obstacle to your development, you have chosen this life and to be in this place. You only have to understand and accept all your choices. When you have accepted them, it will be easier for you to *go home for a visit* and feel the energies that are higher in vibration than those of the Earth. It is the actual higher vibration that makes you long to go there.

Start accepting yourselves as you are, as you look, what you do, your name, your children, your home, and so on. Find your inner happiness and stop searching outside your own body. Have the courage to say out loud what you feel and think to your fellow human beings. Become whole. Every group I meet has virtually the same problems. You don't seek the answers within yourselves, but outside of yourselves. You don't communicate in the right way because you, already at an early stage of your life, at approximately the age of one to three years, when the speech was formed and the language was developed, learned to not say and express your own will. You are all inhibited by your own lives and imprints.

Imprinting

Imprints are, so to speak, inherited from generation to generation, either from the mother or from the father or from both. Often these imprints are passed on unconsciously in generations, and you finally think that they are your own opinions and ideas that you carry. An imprint is something that you house in your physical body which has been transferred on a mental level from your parents. It could be feelings, norms, values, thoughts, opinions, and ideas that are actually not your own, but inherited. Imprints can be hard to find, as they are difficult to discern from one's own burdenings of feelings, experiences, and fears.

The imprint itself is created when the parent's values go against your own inner conception of life. These imprints might create blockages in individuals who cannot discern *their own* values from others'. During your lives, these blockages are then stuck in your physical, emotional, and spiritual bodies and in your psyche.

I usually recommend that you create your own lifeline to work with the imprints.

How will you be able to love your children, the finest you have, with pure and true Love, without imprinting them with guilt, shame, or anxiety? You imprint your children right now the same way you have been imprinted, even though you are aware that you should not act in certain ways. Your own anxiety is transmitted to your children. If you have lived a life of abandonment, how can you then prevent transmitting this feeling to your children?

If you don't feel love for yourself, you cannot love others. How will you be able to open up your heart and send out love to your children if you don't manage to love yourself fully? Is there someone who can give me an answer to this?

Trust

Why do so many of you lack trust? Trust in one's spiritual belief, trust in man, trust in life, trust in birth, trust in one's own life, and so on.

Trust is missing if there is no belief and hope within yourself. Often you are missing the belief that there is another world out there that is other than the one you can see and hear. If you lack trust, you will miss out on all the small miracles that life has to offer you. You miss out on those miracles that we daily try to show you. If the water of life cannot flow freely, then the channels are stopped, and we have difficulties getting through to you. Small, simple things in your everyday life pass you by day after day, and you miss the beauty in life.

If you feel worry and anxiety and don't find the straight road ahead, then stop right away. Do not let this take hold in your bodies. Destructive feelings lead to destructive behaviors that create blockages in your mind. What happens if you are driven by a destructive feeling? Following negative feelings for a long time makes a deep mark and hinders all purification processes within you. You have to understand that the negative thoughts that you are thinking are part of the negative spiral that you send out into the Universe. If you do not believe in your own ability, your own background, and your own origin, a hole emerges within you that makes you feel a lack within yourself, a lack of trust and belief. What you perceive with disgust, fear, or as resistance is a mirror of something inside of you that you have to deal with.

You despise yourself when you despise others around you. Never forget that what you feel most resistance to can offer you the most in your life. Look at people in your surroundings like parts of yourself. The cosmic and spiritual leaders and front figures on Earth do not despise their enemy; they look upon their enemy with warmth. Negative feelings cannot exist in a pure heart.

The day you will be able to stand in front of your enemy and say, "I love you; we have the same origin, the same soul," that day you have full knowledge about life and you are given the opportunity to live here on Earth with a pure heart. Then you are ready to send love to everyone. When trust has turned to knowledge in the depths of your soul, you are ready to open your heart and live with love as a foundation in your life—love for yourself and for everyone in your surroundings, both your friends and your enemies.

When you drift away from your main road, always try to think of your origin and have trust. Believe in yourself, believe in life and that you have protection around you. We help you find your way back to your main road.

The Law of Attraction

There are many texts dealing with the law of attraction. You all know about it—that you should send out what you want, and then you will get it. I cannot completely agree that this is the way it works, but it is true that what you send out is what you attract and get in return, but only if you have a pure, open channel will you get in return what you would call "a wish come true."

Many ask questions like "Why do I not reach my goals? What is it that stops me? Why does everything go wrong in my life?"

It is all about your imprints, memories, and experiences being so strong that they prevent your wish from getting through. They are stronger than your wishes.

It is your imprints, memories, experiences, and destructive patterns you have carried life after life that you send out, and then it is these you attract and get in return. It does not matter if you send out a good thought and wish, when your entire being and your entire soul sends out your negative patterns.

The negative basic patterns that accompany your positive thoughts make your wishes become destructive; you do not get what you wish for. You then believe that these laws do not work.

Many of you think that you have removed the negative in your thoughts, but unfortunately there are many who continue to add the word *not* or another of those negation words in your thoughts and wishes. By doing so, you attract the opposite of what you wish.

You should wish for what you want to achieve, not what you do not want to achieve.

See how easily your wish becomes the opposite of what you want to achieve when you use the word "not." This word does not exist in the higher levels of the Universe.

I do ~~not~~ want to be ill.
I do ~~not~~ want to suffer.
I do ~~not~~ want to be alone.
I do ~~not~~ want to be abandoned.
I do ~~not~~ want to die.

Do you understand?

When you say "not" (I do <u>not</u> want, I do <u>not</u> believe, I am <u>not</u> worthy, and so on), then that is exactly what you send out. The word "not" does not exist in the laws of the Universe. The Universe cannot register the word "not." Think how you think. It is so easy to just leave the word "not" out.

I can ~~not~~ be well.
I am ~~not~~ valuable
I am ~~not~~ well.

Many people do not reach their dreams. Even though they try to affirm and think in the right way, nothing happens. A girl once said to me, "I want a yellow Porsche." I answered her, "If you want a yellow Porsche, then wish for it." Do you think that she got a yellow Porsche? Unfortunately not, because her wish was lower than the obstacles that stood in her way in her unconscious mind. When your wishes are not on a level with your consciousness, they will not be fulfilled.

When you feel a lot of negativity, irritation, and frustration over other people around you, then those are the feelings that you send out, and they will stop you on your way forward on the right path. To avoid this, you must start loving yourself and thereby also automatically everybody else. Then you will never again have a negative thought about yourself or anyone else, not even a rude person. You are all linked in a long chain from the same source. When you love your worst enemy, then you love yourself. Then you, in other words, have no enemy. The law of attraction will then work perfectly, and the girl will get her yellow Porsche.

Peel away all the layers of the onion until you are pure, and only the small seed in the middle is left. It is your own seed, source and origin, the part of you that belongs to God. When all cells, all parts of your body, pulsate with love as a foundation, you can also get what you wish for. When you are totally pure and freed from the negative, it works to send out your innermost wishes. Then, don't be shy, my friends, you can get everything you want.

The Unconscious and Conscious Minds

There are so many things in your lives that you are unaware of, things that reside in the mind that you could call the unconscious. In order to reach this mind, you have to open the key to the subconscious.

Your unconscious mind must go hand in hand with your conscious mind in order for your thoughts and dreams to come true, for you to be able to reach your goals and inner dreams. What is it that has ended up in the unconscious?

It is the kind of things I mentioned earlier: the imprints, thoughts, and feelings that you carry that are not your own. These include imprints and thoughts that have been passed down from your mother and father and their mothers and fathers in many generations. These also include thoughts that your society and your relations carry. You must change your thoughts; you must destroy the feelings that have stagnated in your bodies. These feelings cause disease, violence, and misery on Earth. There is only one true feeling, a fantastic feeling, and that is Love.

When you find your keys by entering the twelve pyramids (see Part 4), you will at the same time regain trust in your own power and

31

knowledge. You will open the door to your unconscious. Let me say it this way: Your bodies are microcosms in a macrocosm. Remember, my friends, that you come from a non-material world into a material one, and then things happen to you. It is now time to return to the material world and to live in a non-material way. In that case, the yellow Porsche might not be the most important thing in life?

You have been separated from your Higher Selves in your sub-conscious and unconscious selves. Now the time is ripe for you to disconnect your brain and live in your heart. To let go of materialism and start to live in a non-material world, even though you are still in a material reality. Every moment that you are in a non-material world and let go of what is physical, which ties you up, you will also receive the keys that open up and set you free to travel in energy and in time. In your dreams and astral travels, you can already now travel unimpeded. This is because you have in this case let go of the body and your brain, the one that ties you to values and thoughts.

The brain is very useful. If you can use both the right and the left halves and master the frequencies of the brain, you can achieve very high intelligence. If you would succeed in connecting your energy pathways between the right and the left hemispheres, you would also have a direct link to your heart and have your consciousness there. Then you would automatically be able to enter your subconscious.

You can never get what you wish for, as long as your unconscious mind and your subconscious mind do not go hand in hand. Your wishes do not become stronger than what your unconscious mind limits you to. You have to cut the strong bond that your unconscious mind has to your brain. The brain should have its strongest bond to the heart; by that you reach your subconscious. You have the opportunity to start when you want. If you knew how simple it is, you would already have done this. It is your brains that make you complicate everything around you.

The Brain

You all know that the brain consists of three parts. The cerebrum masters your thoughts, and a great many people place a lot of focus there. The cerebrum consists of two components: a right half and a left half. The left half works a lot with your analytical mind and your conscious thinking, while the right one works with your creativity and your unconscious thinking. You also have a midbrain, which is the center for your emotions, and the cerebellum, which controls your automatic body functions, such as heart rate, blood pressure, and that which I constantly talk about, the breathing. If you begin to master your breathing, you will at the same time master your cerebellum. When you master the cerebellum, you will master your breathing, and you are then directly synchronized with the sacred inhalation and exhalation of the Cosmos.

I want to give you an inner understanding of how the entire process works together. Your brainwaves send out frequencies; I believe that science talks mostly about five such brainwave frequencies. There are more of them, but there are only five that man has currently demonstrated. When you rise in frequency, you will use other frequencies and waves that are considerably higher, faster in their oscillation, than the Gamma waves that you today consider to be the fastest. The Gamma waves have an oscillation of more than 40 Hz. In the time to come, you will reach significantly higher frequencies than that.

Are you aware that the brain is on all the five levels at the same time? The brain sends out brainwaves in different flows, and the brainwave that dominates at that particular moment is the state of mind that you are in.

The fast impulses are the Gamma waves. They help you to coordinate yourself, your brain and your perception, but they also deal with your memory functions and your higher consciousness.

We move on to the brainwaves for your waking state, those you call Beta waves. These are below 40 Hz. Here you are awake, and the Beta waves help you to focus and concentrate in your everyday life situations. They can also cause a lot of stress and discomfort in your bodies. If you are in a normal unstressed state, you can, by using these waves, concentrate well on the task that you perform.

From Beta we go to the Alpha level, which is the lighter form of relaxation or light meditation. When you reach the Alpha frequency, healing slowly gets started in your body. Here you easily reach your creativity and ability to solve problems. In the Alpha state, you can start to work with the fears in your body, to let the fears and other blockages that prevent you from following your path forward leave you. Right now, it is very important that you learn to master the Alpha waves and to stay on this level, because they help to stimulate both your right and left hemispheres. If you go deeper down in frequency, you lose the opportunity to balance the hemispheres.

Now we move on down to the Theta wave level, which is the deepest form of relaxation before sleep or deep meditation. Here you start to heal on an even deeper level, and here you reach your subconscious thoughts, feelings, blockages, and obstacles that I have spoken so much about with all of you. Here you can, on an even deeper level, continue the work to release fears that hinder you in your development.

The next level is Delta, and these brainwaves are on the lowest frequency, below 4 Hz. This is where you put yourself to sleep. There are humans who are used to deep meditation, who are in very deep Delta but are still in the waking state, but most people sleep. Here you heal your physical body.

It is time to start mastering all these five brainwaves and at any time, at any moment in the waking state, put you in the brainwave frequency that the body needs the most. Learn to balance all five that are all important in their different ways and learn, with just a thought, to be able to tune in to a certain frequency, to in the next moment rise to any of the other frequencies. It will work by itself, it will not be difficult, but I want you to awaken your conscious mind about this.

Frequency and Magnetism

Everything is frequency, motion; everything has a frequency and vibrates in different oscillations. This also means that magnetism is created. A lotus flower vibrates at a higher rate, moves faster, has a higher frequency, than a piece of plastic. Every sound has its fixed, unique frequency. Everything vibrates, from the tiniest cell nucleus to solid mountains. All frequencies create a pattern, and consequently everything that exists has its specific frequency pattern.

Molecules and atoms vibrate, and if they are packed closely together, matter is formed. Matter is frequency, motion. Light creates all sounds, tones create oscillations/frequencies that turn into crystals that are transformed down to Earth, creations are created consisting of light.

Sounds, the tones you hear and the first sound AUM, can be depicted in fantastic frequency patterns as pictures and paintings. If you could see what I see, you would experience that humans create fantastic patterns. The twelve bodies create patterns, all sounds create patterns, and so on. In order to see the patterns, you can put yourself into meditation, reach a trance state, and get an inner image of these to take down.

In the New Age you will develop stronger abilities. You will work with energy, move energy, and even teleport your physical bodies. Other senses will be used for communication. You will use ancient knowledge to work with the ability to turn frequencies into matter, and vice versa. A form of vacuum can be produced to thin out the particles/elements of matter and create a non-solid, subtle form.

Imagine that you add air with as low a frequency as possible between the particles. You change the frequency pulses. This will be important (see Exercises 5 and 6 in Part 3).

Start by observing the frequencies of the Universe, the glowing particles that fall down towards the Earth. Some of you see them daily. They are most easy to see in the morning when the sun is shining and if you peer up on a blue sky. If you enlarge every point of light, you will get crystal in a very high frequency form, not in any solid form. This is a construction material, the material I used myself a long time ago when I built the physical pyramids that were then raised in frequency (Part 4). Each one of you can begin to form these frequencies. Start by perceiving them and playing with them. You will gradually see them indoors and even when it is dark. Within the next few years, you will begin to perceive your outer bodies and the chakra system that resides in the etheric body. Start by cleansing and purifying and then start working with the frequencies in the pyramid system.

Frequency that is densified creates mass. Everything that includes motion has magnetism. The Earth is surrounded by a magnetic field, just as the human body is surrounded by its energy layers, its aura. When the Earth's bodies/energy layers are weakened, it affects the magnetism, which cannot be maintained with its full power. When you have a look at the magnetic field of Earth from above, it reminds you very much of human beings with their energy fields.

The Earth's inner core also consists of magnetism, and the poles of the Earth are held together by it. No collisions against the Earth happen, thanks to this magnetism. When you are holding the negative pole of a magnet against the positive pole of another magnet, they are drawn together, and when you turn one of the magnets, they are repelled.

It is not my intention to give you this form of education, but still, I'd like to speak briefly about changing frequency, moving frequency, and densifying frequency. The frequency which rains down on Earth that you can see with your naked eyes as small snowflakes is possible to pack up, move, and change. I have also spoken about the possibility that exists to move objects. It is only you, yourselves, who at the present moment limit yourselves. Why can you not move your hand through a tabletop? It works the same way as with the magnets mentioned before. Things with the same charge repel each other, while those with differing charge are drawn towards, attract each other. What happens when you try to move your hand through the tabletop? It is repelled. The same principle applies to everything that has motion/frequency. So to be able to move your hand through the tabletop, you simply must change polarity. If you change the polarity of your hand relative to the magnetism, you only have to move your hand through the tabletop. This example does not give you any higher intelligence or knowing, but start playing with this idea; it will benefit you in the future.

The Earth has changed polarity on several occasions during its existence. This includes north and south poles turns, changing places, but also turning back. So if you change polarity in your physical body, then you will be able to do what we are talking about—move in time and space. You remember what I said: That which is not matter consists of air, right? If you pack matter and air together, you will have a solid object, mass. If you fill it up with additional air, then it will be easier to reduce the magnetism. When the motion inside the object stops, the magnetism decreases, and you have access to change the polarity so that the objects are repelled or meet. You can start to play with these skills and with the idea.

The seasons are of importance when you work with frequencies. Certain seasons strengthen certain frequencies. The pyramids and the celestial bodies are affected by the seasons. When the climate is upside down, the physical body becomes weaker and is more easily exposed to health problems.

If the poles are moved (the north and south poles) the magnetism, of course, is weakened, and the Earth can be exposed. This has happened several times during the Earth's existence. For that reason, we have a pyramid (number 9), whose task is to balance and protect the poles.

Believe in Your Own Power

It is now time to awaken the trust in yourself and your abilities, trust in who you really are. If you do not realize what great potential, magic, and power you are going to acquire, it does not matter how many times you enter the pyramids. If you do not have trust that you evolve and that it happens quickly, you will not be able to think along those lines that give you the magic. Just realize that you are reading this publication for a reason and that your subconscious has brought you to this book to listen to an old man like me. I give you a slight kick in the pants so that you open up your eyes and see what power you yourself have and that you have all answers within you. As the keys open up every pyramid, I will be superfluous. Then I will just come down to visit you for a cup of coffee, or whatever you call it. Maybe then many of you will be able to see me with your physical eyes or with your inner physical vision. Soon we will be on the same plane, on the same level, so that you can see me with your physical eyes, not just feel me.

You have lost your trust because of your adaptation, so now your self-esteem has to be rebuilt so that you realize what potential you have, what wonderful individuals you are. When you are healed, Mother Earth will be healed, and at the same time you will open channels to higher and higher etheric information that exists. If one of your individuals is healed, then all are healed. If all are healed on every plane, then all are completely healed. Look upon it as ripples on water. Make an affirmation every morning to yourself: "I trust in myself and my ability."

Thoughts

What is the first thing you think of when you wake up in the morning? I wish that everyone would think "A wonderful new day," but unfortunately, this is not the case. Begin the day by thanking for waking up to a new beautiful day. You have to change your thoughts in order to change your patterns from scratch and for the transformation to take place in each one of you. Remember that every day, when the frequencies are raised, your thoughts are sent out and they just keep getting stronger. What you wish for is what rebounds back to each one of you. You have to believe in yourself; believe in your power and the magic you can create in your physical being.

It is time, starting now, to send out pure thoughts. You can never send out a pure thought to someone else if it is not preceded by a pure thought to yourself. How many of you think healthy thoughts about yourself every minute of the hours of the day, even during your dreamtime? This is the first transformation that must occur, and on that occasion the greatest change will also happen. You can only create this change by an active work to transform every dark and negative thought. You have heard this before, but too many do not live up to this.

It is time to see beyond the small things to reach the big things. You could say that your physical beings are a micro universe from a macro cosmic perspective. So everything that goes on in a small cell in your body is an identical copy of what is going on in the process of creation of the Universe. When you begin to see from a wider perspective, you can also begin to let go of the small things around you, to realize that everything has a purpose. Everything has a meaning, and nothing happens by accident. The forces, which are started in conjunction with the frequency increases, are so enormous, and exist on a level beyond your comprehension, because your thoughts limit you.

Humans must stop thinking negatively. Every time you send out a negative thought to a fellow human being or to yourself, it is reflected straight in and bounces back to you. This means that when you feel negative energies from another human being, it is your own deepest subconscious anger that you feel.

You will never learn to love and forgive, as long as you cannot love (if I may call it that) your worst enemy. In order to reach this high love, you also must learn to love yourself, because everything starts with yourself. Every negative thought you send out means that you do not love yourself or trust yourself and your ability.

Many Earth humans choose to live their lives with anger, frustration, hate, desire, and power, and they step on others to satisfy their desires and acquire greater power. It is time for you humans to now, in this time, in this moment, realize that you in the depth of yourselves also belong to these people, with all people on all levels, whether you perceive them as good or as less pleasant. This means that you shall embrace everyone and let go of the thought of I, the power of your ego, and instead think We; what can We do?

39

To Practice What One Teaches—
To Be in the Now

I have earlier spoken about how you should purify and bless your food. If you know that the food you put in you is not pure, can you then reach higher wisdom by eating it? Many do not follow their hearts. You know that you eat a product that contains toxins, dangerous fats, and other impurities, but still you put it in your mouth. Even though you can now use the power of the thirty-six sacred frequencies that exist in the Universe to purify and heal the food, you choose to go against the true self, yourself. You have not developed any wisdom concerning your knowledge about diet.

This also applies to many other activities in your lives. You do not honor your bodies, but choose to add toxins, even when you have the choice not to. When higher knowledge reaches love, that is the heart, and you practice what you teach—then, my friends, you are wise.

For a long, long time I just sat in darkness doing nothing, just acquiring wisdom. I really did nothing but sit in the dark to receive answers and to grow. As I sat in the darkness I had no external stimulus, and by being without stimuli, I ultimately found the answers. I grew and found my inner and outer vision; my range and ability to take in from nothing. Solitude and silence lead to the very highest form of understanding. Then miracles and wonders can be achieved. Thereafter I went out on Earth and acted in accordance with this knowledge, from the heart, and showed what true wisdom was. This was thousands of years ago, and it is now your turn to do the same.

Now many of you think, "Well, I have done this, and I have eaten like that," but you should not think of what has been. In that case, you put guilt and shame on yourself and create new blockages. Then you have not understood anything of the wheel I am trying to teach you about.

You are only here and now. From now on, you are reborn; nothing that you have done exists. Let go of yesterday, my friends. You are here and now. It can be easy to live, but many people make it very difficult. Every negative feeling that arises within you, you have the right to feel, because you are in the now when the feeling comes, but you also have to let go of it. Because tomorrow, there is no yesterday. This means that you must let go of the negative feeling before tomorrow is reborn. In this way, you will not get any new blockages preventing your development.

Micro and Macro Cosmos

As I said in the beginning of my story, everything in your physical body is identical with the creation of the Universe, everything in the human body is an image of how the process of creation came about at the birth of the Universe. When you were descended into physical form, a replica of the creation process of the Universe was simultaneously created in each individual. You are also all linked together in a string of pearls, where you all have a bond to every other human now living on Earth and to all souls who earlier have had a connection to Earth. You are connected like rings in rings. Everything you do and think affects all others through this string of pearls. The string connects you all the way up to what I call Prime Creator, that which others call God, Allah, or the like.

You often forget to gather knowledge from all earlier experiences you have had in other forms of existence. I said earlier that time does not exist, that it is an illusion. If it does not exist, you may find yourself on all planes, in all locations simultaneously. What you see, do, and feel is a direct mirror image fed back to you from this or any other existence.

All of you, all of humanity, have a connection to Prime Creator and a connection to Mother Earth. When you forget this connection and send out negative thoughts to others around you, these thoughts are reflected back like a mirror image to you and discredit you. You are all individuals on the planet interconnected, and this means that when groups of people and societies suffer and feel bad, this is mirrored to you, and you also feel bad inside your microcosm. When you feel bad in your microcosm, then the macrocosm feels bad. When the macrocosm feels bad, then the microcosm feels bad.

If you instead balance, heal, and purify yourself on all planes, then a lot of other individuals and large groups will also feel better. When you feel good in your microcosm, then the macrocosm feels good. When the macrocosm feels good, then the microcosm feels good. It is about finding balance in life by finding love for yourself, to love yourself. Understand that you are a holy individual and that every human is as beautiful and wonderful as you.

You can never love another human being if you don't love yourself fully. In order to achieve this, you have to open up your unconscious. Start to listen to your intuition in all situations and in all choices you face from all directions in life. It is good if you can be in a middle plane energetically, both be grounded in the planet and be highly vibrating with connection to Prime Creator. Then you live as humans and care for the Earth and all its forms of existence, at the same time as you open up for higher knowledge. Be just as much in the higher energies as in Mother Earth's energy. It is time to start living in the heart. It is time to start loving yourself. To be able to love any other human being, another living individual, and Mother Earth, you must love yourself and have an understanding for the origin of existence, Prime Creator.

Remember that during the year, all your thoughts will manifest. Then, what do you do, all you Earth humans, when you wake up in the morning thinking "I am ugly; I am fat and not worth anything." You carry the wrong pictures and do not understand or remember that each one of you is a unique, highly developed soul who carries all knowledge and truth. You can make a choice, starting today, to experience and love yourself and only send out positive thoughts to those around you. Every time you doubt, turn a positive thought to yourself. Go and have a look at yourself in the mirror, deep into your eyes; see your soul and realize that it is adaptation that has made you lose the thread.

Adaptation

The ability to adapt is very high in each one of you when you are born into an earthly life and have to adapt there. Adaptation is an ability that has to exist, for you to even be able to enter a human body and become a human being. This is an ability that affects you deeply on all levels. But adaptation has also created lots of traumas in each one of you, traumas that can be processed in what I call the lifeline. These traumas are created by you having adapted to everything that happens during life. You adapt to your family, your parents, your school environment, your work, different places, people, circumstances, and situations in such a high degree that you have forgotten to follow the message of your heart.

You are born with the ability to follow your inner voice and to do something specific in your life. But your ability to adapt made you lose communication with your inner self, that is, your Higher Self. You lost trust in yourself and your own ability. That is why you ended up on the side paths that I spoke about earlier. You do not find your way back up on the main road that will lead you to the right work and the knowledge that you shall acquire in this time.

Already, in the early years of childhood, far too many turn off their contact with Prime Creator and with Mother Earth. You have been adapted, based on the needs of your near and dear ones, right from early childhood, long before your communication and linguistic development started, when you still were unable to express yourself with words. Many children do not even have the opportunity to express "No." They are not heard and seen for who they are.

All parents unconsciously bring their children into a phase of adaptation during the time of their upbringing. This is because you are born with the ability to adapt and because it is a must. The little child is shaped and adapts itself in all environments outside the home as it grows up. He or she adapts to friends, partners, work, and so on, until adulthood. The adaptation never ends. Finally, the connection to your ability to reach in to your inner voice is broken. You do not follow that which was your road, your path to walk to reach the highest potential, the highest truth, and the highest development that you were intended for in this particular earthly life.

In every situation you face, in every circumstance you end up in from this moment on, here and now, you should question your inner Self, your heart, whether this is what you want, if this is where you are going, and if this is helping you today, now. This means that you will slowly, day by day, second after second, here and now, be able to live focused and let go of the adaptation that doesn't follow your own inner voice. This will set you free and will help to raise you so that you get access to the twelve keys and all knowledge in the twelve pyramids.

I have seen humans who have adapted to everything and everybody, from start to finish. They have completely lost themselves. Do you recognize this?

When you let go of adaptation, and all that which you have been shaped to after not following your inner voice, you can use the Line (see Part 3). Write down everything you remember, perceive, and feel, and then burn the paper. Let go! Live here and now, from now on. Never, ever look back. This means that what has been, does not exist anymore. It is time for you to start focusing on who you are, your mission, and where you want to go in life. In order for you to get this connection with yourself, there is only one way to go, and that is to follow what you call intuition, your sixth sense. Ask yourself, "Who am I? What am I? What do I want? What goals do I have in my life? What is the meaning of my life?"

I get these questions very often, but it is you, humans, who have the mission in life to follow your inner voice and shape yourselves into individuals who live in harmony and in your full power. You also must use the abilities that you have brought with you and acquired during various lives. Here and now, in the body you have received, you accept who you are and follow your inner voice. There is only one way to go, and that is to follow your sixth sense, your intuition.

Intuition

What is intuition? Gut feeling, many of you would probably answer. But it is rather a sensation where information is created to thoughts totally without interference from the brain. Such a sensation is a direct contact with your heart, your subconscious, with Prime Creator and Mother Earth. When you get this kind of sensation, you experience it as a feeling in the body, and you cannot be mistaken that it is an intuitive feeling, something that is not originating from the mental activity of the brain.

Your gut feeling, however, can often fool you, through the adaptation that your ego and your unconscious mind have taught you to follow. The brain constructs appropriate responses that come like chains of thought; one thought gives rise to the next, and so on. Your adapted and unconscious mind follows the encoded "sense of reason" that you have learned is "right." You are adapted to be "reasonable" according to norms and regulations that have been passed on from generation to generation, in life after life. This leads to you wandering about on side paths, instead of walking straight forward on the main road towards the goal you are destined for.

Feelings of Guilt

Now we will talk a little about feelings of guilt. Why do you feel so much guilt? What do you feel guilty for? Who or what gives you these feelings of guilt? If guilt exists, then what is it?

Guilt is something that you have been imprinted to feel, through many generations on Earth.

Guilt is a destructive feeling that affects your bodies. Guilt does not exist if you do not believe in it yourself. Trust what I say. Trust that guilt is only a feeling that has been created by humans on Earth, totally without reason and higher purpose. It was constructed only for the purpose of suppressing and dominating the people who live there.

Instead of adding to your feelings of guilt when you have done something that you feel in your soul is wrong, you should ask yourself, "Why did I do that? What is the source of this action?" When the answer reveals itself, forgive yourself and move on. Feel no guilt. Guilt creates anxiety. You have nothing to feel guilty about. Your actions are just a part of human life. Forgive yourself. If you do not forgive yourself, you can never forgive your fellow human beings.

The little child is born totally innocent, beautiful, and pure, and is then formed into an adult. The child is formed by its parents, who in turn have been formed by their parents, and so on, in a long, long chain. Start by emptying the little child's burdenings from generations and you will see that you can reach your own source.

Abandonment and Loneliness

Abandonment is a feeling that I know many children get to experience, and this leaves deep scars in their souls, even if the feeling originates from past lives. To grow up with a feeling of being abandoned, unwanted, and to no use, leaves very deep scars. The feeling of abandonment leaves scars just as deep as those left by feelings of guilt, shame, anxiety, worry, and so on. The feeling of abandonment creates in many of you an imprint that follows you all the way into adulthood and may lead to difficulties for you to deal with loneliness. It is only you yourself who can change these deep marks by filling yourself with love. You must love yourself to be able to move on from where you are today.

Dear children, you have never been abandoned. What has been abandoned in your lives is trust and contact with your origin, the Source. There has always been love around you and always will be.

Many of you feel a strong loneliness, even though you live in a partner relationship. The reason for this is that you have lost contact and communication with your Higher Self and are longing for it. Others may not experience this feeling of loneliness, in that they live in a partner relationship. But a partner is only an illusion to suppress the feeling of absence of, and separation from, your Higher Self. Somewhere during the process of reincarnation, in your chain of collection of experiences, you have begun to adopt a feeling and a belief that you are depending on other individuals to feel satisfaction, love, and affinity. Where does the feeling of love come from?

Along the way, your view of the origin of love has been distorted so that you look upon it as an *external feeling* that must come *to* you instead of an *internal feeling* that will come from *within*. If you must have acknowledgment from outside to feel love, then you have not experienced the basic feeling of love. In adulthood, you must give yourself acknowledgment, attention, consideration, and love. The little child is depending on the attention of the grown up, but as adults you yourselves have to be responsible to replenish yourselves. In order to move on with your lives and your developmental process, you must from now on realize that you are not alone, even though you feel that way. You belong to the All and to the chain that connects all of you together.

Again, loneliness is an untrue truth that has been added to you in your early childhood days in connection with the starting of adaptation. Realize that you never, ever would have needed to be alone if you had been allowed to follow your heart. Loneliness is a human invention and actually does not exist. When you have fully grasped the process of creation, that all humans are connected like a chain, you will understand that you are never alone, regardless of whether you live with a partner or not.

Why don't you humans have any deep fellowship, a unity consciousness? You believe that you are separated and lonely. You do not own the knowledge that you are all one. When you feel loneliness, what you feel is an imprint that has been learned. You have learned to believe that loneliness, an empty space, arises when you do not have a relationship. If you think this way about relationships, it is proof of the fact that loneliness does not exist, but is created by man. There is so much created by man that doesn't exist in the original creation. Start traveling and visit each other if you need company. On the astral plane, you have the opportunity to travel whenever you want, wherever you want.

In adulthood, love and acknowledgment have to come to you from yourself. Other people can only send out a sensation of love to you, in the form of feelings and thoughts, hoping that they themselves will have this sensation in return. It is merely love for yourself that you first must feel in order to understand the unconditional in true Love, that which is the origin of all other feelings. You always have to start with yourself.

You are a unique individual, and you can never take for granted that other people will be able to read and feel your thoughts and feelings. Everybody has unique experiences and patterns.

Already during the time of Atlantis the connections up to Prime Creator and down to Earth began to decline, and finally they were cut off. The connection with your sixth sense was erased, and knowledge about the Origin was lost. Many of your tales of life in Pyramid 3 have been about bringing back these lost parts. Life after life, many of you have wandered about without finding the thread that leads to the opening of the heart and the subconscious mind. Enter the third pyramid and remake your lifeline. Enter and change and work with the feelings that hinder you right now. Everything is a creation story of imagination and myth.

Choices

You face so many choices in life. It makes me so tired when I see how many choices you are faced with. During my whole life on Earth, I do not think I was faced with as many choices as you do during one day. How are you supposed to make the right choices if you cannot follow your intuition? When you make the wrong choices, you end up on the wrong path and might even live the life of someone else. This creates disease, disharmony, anxiety, worry, and stress.

Everything begins with the beautiful feeling of Love. Many other feelings mostly mess things up for you. You close down your emotional life because of unpleasant things that you have encountered in life. In order to set you free, these unpleasant things must surface. To release, purify, and dare to face your feelings is unpleasant. All children are born pure, with the highest knowledge within themselves, and all children carry the knowledge which I try to help you to open up. Life should be simple, but has become complicated because of all your feelings.

Love

What is Love? It is the highest, purest energy. Love is your origin and what you call the power of God. You are all connected to Prime Creator and this power. You are Love. When you see a little newborn baby, you experience a feeling that outweighs everything else. The feeling you experience in that moment is true, pure Love. It is unconditional and very deep and makes you shed tears of happiness. In such moments you can feel exactly what I mean when I say that the truth comes from within, you feel that it exists within you.

I can tell you that I have experienced earthly love myself in this way. It is fantastic, as close to the original Love as you can achieve on Earth among all sorrow and pain. However, it is just a fraction of the Divine Love. In my world, the purest Love exists in all situations, in all circumstances, always. How will you get there? How will you break the patterns you have been imprinted by and the forms you have been molded in? How will you change things? How do you break old patterns? How will you be able to take a step back and release your shackles? How will you be able to give love to your children, if you don't know what pure Love is?

To love oneself is the prerequisite for all other forms of love. To find love for yourself, you have to start by finding the little child in yourself that perhaps did not get the love it needed during the first important years.

You have many blockages from your early childhood years that must be resolved. It is painful not to be seen, not to be acknowledged, not to be heard. Bring forth the little child in you and give love to yourself.

Cradle the child within you. See how you cradle the little child who is you, how you comfort and take care of it. Give yourself that which you did not get the first years of your life, when you were dependent on love from your closest ones. If necessary, make an affirmation every day to yourself that you are valuable, that you are good enough as you are, and that you are fine. Now that you are a grownup, you have the opportunity to give yourself what you lack. If it is homesickness you feel, travel home. What are you waiting for? Go for a visit, and fill yourself up with the frequencies of your home.

If it is love that you miss in yourself—fill yourself up with love. If you want to let go of imprints, then do so. Learn to let go of old imprints that you carry and injustices that you have been exposed to in both this life and others. Peel the onion, so to speak, remove layer after layer. Realize your own ability, and bring forth love for yourself.

The problem is that many of you hold on so tight to things, that the ability to let go is blocked. You hold on to people, relationships, events, belongings, and other things, long after you should have let go of them. Or sometimes you on the contrary let go too quickly, to avoid feelings of injustice. You must realize that you cannot let go of these things if you do not want to admit that you have them. When you hold on to imprints, fears, old injustices, and so on, you may end up becoming bitter, destructive, and filled with anxiety. Bitterness, negativity, and anxiety are what eventually lead to physical disease.

It is all about recognizing the patterns. They are shaped as nets around you. It is about having the courage to go into your own pain. If you do not see the patterns, it is not possible to break them. You must dare to go into your patterns of fears, even though it is painful. In an organized form, it is possible to arrange through meditation, consultations, conversations, and so on, but the most fantastic form is the one you can create yourself. Go into deep relaxation, go into every layer you have within you, and reach the pain on every level. It is your fears that limit you from reaching your pain. You are afraid that it will hurt, even more than it did when you once experienced the pain. Work on yourself. You must give yourself time, time to dissolve that which hurts.

If you now, in adulthood, still live with destructive feelings and patterns from your early childhood years, it is not enough with only one try to get rid of them. You must be determined and try over and over again. You are all aware of some of your negative imprints, negative webs that you have spun around you against your will. Go into all negative experiences that you believe are the reason that you cannot feel and give love fully, with the awareness that "You are grown up now and can handle these feelings." And ask yourself, "Why do I suffer from this? How will I be able to give love? How will I get rid of my anxious body, my restless mind? How do I get rid of my fears? How will I love myself? How will I forgive? How will I as a grownup be able to break this? What is the worst thing that can happen to me?" Go on asking the same questions over and over again, until that which hurts and is painful is gone. Until the anxiety has disappeared. Until the guilt and the shame and all the negative feelings no longer exist. Until you feel a purity. It is this purity that I call Source. In the beginning it feels like an emptiness, but then it turns into a feeling of purity. That is where you then find true Love.

Begin already tonight when you go to sleep. Begin to remove, cleanse, and go into yourself to reach deeper, into the subconscious web that exists within you. The subconscious layers are the layers that you do not know, those you are not aware of. You can either get very clear or very subtle notions about feelings, events, reactions, or other signals that reflect earlier events and experiences. You will be able to feel deep anxiety, sorrow, anger, and fear, because these were the feelings you had when you were mistreated or violated. Enter into this feeling of anxiety, sorrow, anger, or fear and the feelings of discomfort that it again causes you. Re-experience them, and go deeper into them. Stay in the feeling and say to yourself, "I now let go of this feeling; I do not need it anymore. I forgive myself for being blind." In that you forgive, you let go of injustices and imprints. When you have made this journey over and over again, you will experience that you are increasingly able to love and forgive yourself. That's what this is all about: love and forgiveness.

51

If you have problems and difficulties with loving yourself, it is nice if you can work a lot with the tenth pyramid (see Part 4). I say it again: Open your hearts and send out true Love. When you have succeeded in sending out this Love once, it will be easier to do it a second time, third time, and so on, until it creates a positive pattern in your entire being; you become Love.

Forgiveness

How many of you are in your heart satisfied with your looks? How many of you look at yourself in the mirror every morning and say, "Oh, how beautiful I am! What a fantastic soul." If only you knew what fantastic individuals you all are. If only you knew what great beings you are and how holy every one of you is. What you see in the mirror is only a shell that you have borrowed and stay in for a short moment. If you look deep into your eyes, you can get a glimpse of your greatness, your soul.

How many times every day do you think a negative thought about your neighbor? Or react negatively to someone's clothing, their home, their way of being, and so on. Dear friends, in order to be healed on the deepest level, the first step is to let go of all negative thoughts. As I have already mentioned many times, all individuals on the planet are interlinked in a long chain and affect each other. This means that every negative thought that you send out will immediately come back to you as a mirror image. In this way, you violate yourself over and over again.

There is only one true feeling, and that is love. How many feelings do you have each day that have nothing to do with love? Many, haven't you? Have you ever asked yourself where they come from? What lies behind your thoughts is what I have told you over and over again—your adaptation and your imprints. You are not taught when you are young that you are fantastic. Instead, many of you grow up with feelings of guilt, shame, anxiety, and condemnation of yourselves. Peel all this away and you will regain contact with yourself.

The next step is to go through a purification process of forgiveness. By that I mean forgiveness of yourself. All that you have been through, both what you have exposed yourself to and what you have allowed others to expose you to, must be forgiven. Forgive yourself that your consciousness has been clouded and that you did not have the knowledge, understanding, or ability to defend yourself from being exposed. You must learn to forgive yourself so that you can forgive all people around you that you ever sent a negative thought to.

It is not until you love your enemies that you will love yourself and understand what deep and true Love is. Learning how to forgive always starts by forgiving yourself. Forgive yourself for exposing your soul to be born in a body where you have experienced shame, guilt, anxiety, worry, and other such things. You can forgive yourself for putting yourself into this situation.

But always remember that the plan for your life was created before you were born. All of you have thoroughly gone through your basic plan and what you are supposed to learn during this earthly life. Many of you have planned, as one of your missions in life, to break negative patterns that you have carried in life after life. Another mission is to learn how to find true Love. True Love is needed on Earth here and now. Your planet is about to fall to pieces. There is so much misery and negativity on your Earth. The more humans who find their way back to Prime Creator, the love for themselves and their children, and break their negative patterns, the larger is the number that also will be able to help with the great work we have ahead of us. This is a work that has already been started. To be able to heal with the power of Prime Creator, the highest healing power, you have to be pure yourself.

The fourth pyramid, Atlantis, is among other things about forgiveness. You have the opportunity to enter the pyramid and ask to undergo a process of forgiveness of everything that has influenced you to not live in the power and greatness that you have.

You have all the answers inside of you. Through the Matrix of the twelve pyramids, you reach the keys that give you access to that which you have forgotten. To reach forgiveness, to find love, and to live in the heart are the three main steps to access the keys and all knowledge inside of you. In order to manage the three main steps, you must learn to let go of things that burden you. It is only you yourself who can go in and do it; nobody else can do it for you. If there is no time, there is no yesterday either. This means that these things that you will let go of do not actually exist.

Focus your thoughts with a clear intention to live in the now, the only moment that exists. Old events will then be able to fade away. To gain understanding, the most important thing for each of you is to learn that you presently are in a material world, but that you actually are non-material, and that the ego is an image of your physical self. The ego gives you an identity and individuality on the physical plane.

It is so simple when you understand the technique and when it dawns on you how everything works. You will let go of old traumas from many incarnations in just an instant, and your children will give birth to children that grow up without guilt, shame, and anxiety.

Get to work tonight, and you will in a short time feel like you were born again. Many times, you will think about why you have not done this before. Please write down what you experience and feel, so that you can easily return to these feelings if it is needed to continue to let go.

After purification, it is important to learn to never add new burdenings in your body. Fill yourself with light and love after each time you let go of something.

Remember that all humans are good. It is only the environment that makes humans have undesirable behaviors. These are their imprints.

Karma

At the same time as Atlantis fell, that which you call karma was created. But what is karma? It is an illusion, my friends! You would never during this long time have had to live with karma if you had allowed your hearts to be open. If you had allowed the link to the Mother and to the Father, the Sun, and Prime Creator to be open. Thanks to the Matrix, the link has always been available. But as I just started to tell you, you have been imprinted in the belief that you must live with obstacles and blockages in generation after generation after generation …

The first questions I get from all humans I meet are "What is the meaning of my life? Why am I here? What is my higher purpose?" My friends, you will find the answer in the pyramid matrix and in the frequency of the Atlantean pyramid (see Part 4). That which you call karma, meaning deeds you have done in a life that you think have to be justified so that things will work out better for you after death and you will live a better life next time, is an illusion. All along, it has just been an illusion that was created to keep man in check.

The phenomenon of karma was created because in Atlantis there were higher energies, individuals, who misused the forces, and this broke the camel's back. This contributed to the fall of Atlantis and to various impairments. This does not mean that you can act however you like without repercussions. Absolutely not. There are laws in the Universe that you can never ignore. A law of karma does not exist, but there is a law of cause and effect. What you give is what you get in return. Like a mirror image. You do not have to live a life in order to make up for another one. But you get what you give. So it is actually quite simple, but man has misunderstood this law and this system. Everything has two poles, light/darkness, feminine/masculine, yin/yang, and so on. The purpose of these is that they shall balance each other up to a harmonious wholeness.

The hierarchies of society have disturbed man for thousands of years. The strong hierarchical order that you have on Earth does not exist anywhere else in the Universe. The law that I call cause and effect is now strengthened day by day on Earth. The stronger this law becomes, the more changes will happen in society and its structures.

The hierarchies are about to loosen up. This means that you have to give up the materialistic way of living and your consumption. Man speaks about possessions as uplifting things, which he believes strengthen him and make him important. The law means that every action and thought that you send out, goes directly back to you. Therefore, it is important that you give unconditionally, without a thought or an ulterior motive to get something in return. The one who does not own anything, but still gives unconditionally of the little he or she has, is the one who is called master and carries the knowledge.

When one gives out of nothing, one creates abundance at the same time. Is abundance money, castles with pinnacles and towers? Abundance is when you live in total balance, harmony, presence, and unconditional love. In that the structures of society are about to dissolve, communication with mobiles and computers will also come to an end. Understand, develop, and utilize the telepathic ability that you all carry.

At all times, individuals and civilizations have entered the Earth plane contrary to the principles of the highest council. The same law applies to them. It rebounds back on them and their system. Everything is connected in a universal system. In such a system, Earth is a microcosm.

If you act from your heart and follow the principles that are genuine, you will not harm or disharmonize other objects, individuals, or other living beings. With the frequency Earth is in at the moment, it is a big challenge to manage to live in the heart. Many of you don't do that, but ignore the Higher Self, truth, intuition, and consciousness, and the only ones that are affected by this are you yourselves. Many of you then choose, and have chosen for thousands of years, to go down to Earth over and over again to create a life where you follow the values that you have within yourselves from Prime Creator.

If you misuse or do something that is looked upon as less positive, there is nothing that says that it does not have a purpose that is beneficial. What is good and what is bad, and who can judge what is good or bad?

Light, Darkness, and Evil

In the Atlantean pyramid, a battle between light and darkness started. Light and darkness are each other's opposites, the feminine and the masculine power. Neither can exist without the other. But man has created what you call evil, and you associate it with darkness. Think how wrong things have gone during many generations. So many children who unnecessarily have been born with fear of darkness. Have you thought about that—why a child is born with fear of darkness? A child who has an open heart and has acquired a high level of knowledge. This is because the imprinting has already started. It is not the child's own fear, but an imprint from the parents and earlier generations.

What will you do then to let go of that which you call evil, the dark around you? Step into the darkness, forgive, and embrace. To enter the darkness is, of course, step one. What you are afraid of in the darkness is aspects of yourself. You are faced with things from times when you have not acted from your heart, when you have thought and acted separate from your heart, where your ego has controlled the thoughts of your brain. You are afraid of yourself. Enter, embrace, and realize that the darkness is just as bright as the light. It is all the fears you are carrying that create a darker darkness. It is only you yourself who creates and attracts what you call less positive energies. Everywhere around you there is energy, you are made of energy. If you are afraid of the energy, then you are afraid of yourself. But if there is no darkness, why then is there so much evil, you wonder. I have touched this subject a few times. What is evil? Who judges what is good and evil?

Just the idea that you own the capacity to judge if someone or something is evil has made you strengthen your ego. Then you look upon yourself and your own actions as better than anyone else. When you are going to live in your heart, you have to do it fully. Step one is "Do not judge any human being, for then you judge yourself."

Everything starts with a thought. Let go of your thoughts and only live in love. I feel like a preacher, priest, or the like, and that was not my intention. But no matter how we turn this thing over in our minds, I still want to stimulate thoughts in you about what is good and what is evil. Is there no evil? Is there no good? Who controls the Universe, my friends? Who is Prime Creator? It is you, each and every one of you. You are all linked together in a long spiral, all the way up to Prime Creator. You are a part of that which you call the divine power, aren't you? If each and every one of you is divine and holy, then there are no obstacles anymore for any of you to free yourself from everything around you.

We were talking about evil. No human being needs to return into physical form to make up for something from an earlier event or from a past life, but one gets to experience and endure what one has created and done to others and oneself. Who owns the right to set themselves up as a judge of what is right and wrong? Of course there are such things you are never allowed to do, such as breaking the fundamental laws of the Universe. But certain events happen and will happen to teach people something or to create energies and other things that are necessary on Earth at the time. Events that have been predetermined for a long time and which are a pawn in the great game. Everybody creates their truth, their own myth and illusion.

Going into yourself, your inner darkness, sets you free from imprints and blockages. You'll reach inner knowledge and wisdom. This makes you grow from within. Silence and solitude in a meditative state makes you grow and increases your knowledge.

The Pyramid of Cheops

Have you ever wondered how the sacred Pyramid of Cheops was built? Do you think that they used a pick and shovel? To create something that amazing they used sound and light, a higher vibratory level, what you call a higher dimension, and also energy pathways and meridians. This applies to many buildings that still exist today in physical form, but the etheric pyramids were also created in this way.

Meridians are energy pathways that are needed to create with the power of thought and with the sound and light of crystal. I want you to again start opening up to this knowledge and take it back. When some co-workers and I built the Pyramid of Cheops as the physical image of the twelve etheric pyramids, we got to use these pathways. When you are to create, this can happen on a higher level than the one you find yourself on. If you create on a higher frequency and then lower that which you have created to the frequency you find yourself in, you can create everything you want. All you need to do is to transform down and densify the energy, so that it becomes more and more compact and solid, until you have created matter.

There is a method on Earth where you measure the age of objects and decide how old they are. If you would do this with the stones that are left in the pyramid, you would find that the oldest stone is at the top. It does not matter which stone you start to build with, if you master the law of gravity. You all carry with you the knowledge to master the law of gravity. Who said that the bottom has to be built before the top? It is only you humans who have created this obstacle to you. Many of the obstacles you carry with you were created during the Atlantean era.

The Twelve Layers of the Human Body

Your energy field, what you call the aura, consists of twelve energy layers, including your physical body. Seven of these layers are more dense and five are more subtle. All the cells in the body are constructed in the same way, of twelve both physical and subtle parts. Many other teachers have said that you consist of five, seven, or ten layers or bodies, but according to me there are twelve in number. For you to easier understand my explanation, I will use the bodies and their names that many of you already know and add two bodies that until now have been unknown to you. The bodies are structured in layers on layers outside each other, like the layers of an onion. The layers surround and go through your physical bodies and interact with each other, like in an integrated communication system. They are each also connected with their respective chakra and etheric pyramid.

I will give you a short description here of these different bodies. It is important for you to understand that you are more than what you can see with your eyes. The human being is in its construction a copy of the process of creation. The understanding of the descending transformation is important in your evolution. I will describe the twelve layers in the order you were created, starting from Prime Creator.

Layer 12. The Atmic Body: There is actually no correct name for this layer, but the most appropriate is the Atmic body. This is the outermost layer of your being, the outermost of your bodies, that which merges with the All, Prime Creator. It is imperceptible, because it has such a high frequency. It has a direct link or connection in to the abode of the soul, where the soul seed resides. This abode is located in your body in the space between the pericardium and the heart. Thus, the soul energy is not situated in your heart but surrounds it, while the pericardium serves as a vessel for your heart and your soul energy.

The Atmic body is a drop of Prime Creator. It is this drop that surrounds those layers that lie inside, those that create bodies that are more and more dense in their energies. The word Atman comes from the original language Sanskrit and means soul energy, that which permeates everything and is indestructible. This body contains the pattern for duality, the cosmic law that makes it possible for things to manifest and for matter to eventually be created. The Atmic body consists of pure soul energy.

Layers 6-11. The Metapersal Body: This body with its layers is the original fabric of man as a creation, without failings and faults; that is, the perfect human. The fabric is transformed down to a denser and denser frequency level through the layers of the Metapersal body. Here does not yet exist any I-form nor instincts and desires. The body contains all stored information from creation, the Big Bang.

The outermost layers of the Metapersal body are possible to view from above, but cannot be perceived by man himself. The layers are so subtle that no light can be reflected on them, and therefore you cannot perceive them.

The inner layers of the Metapersal body may be perceived in connection with lightwork. In the New Age you will start to perceive these bodies more clearly. Here duality is manifested and polarity comes into existence. From the patterns of the Atmic body, forms can begin to be created. These layers contain the finished basic pattern for the next step in your descending transformation. Now the next body can be manifested.

Layer 5. The Causal Body: Here are the codes for your mental, emotional, and physical abilities and heredity factors from all of your existences. It is these codes that create the pattern for the individual human. Here your Higher Self consciousness and the first outpost for what you call the ego reside. This is the first layer where one can express "I am," "I exist," and "I am an individual." This body and the next, the Mental body, contain the patterns for all of the individual's experiences and lessons from all existences.

Layer 4. The Mental Body: The Mental body is sensitive to impressions from the soul and is an intermediary between the lower and the higher bodies. Here your thoughts are created and born, both the concrete and the abstract. Feelings and thoughts here have a higher frequency and thereby also have a higher quality, so to speak, than feelings and thoughts in the next body (the Astral body). The Mental body can be seen as connected with the previous body, the Causal body.

Layer 3. The Astral Body: This body is often called the Emotional body and drives the motion of energies in your body. It is the place for your emotions, the ones connected to your earthly activities and attitudes. This body also controls your instincts and desires that can be totally earthbound or of a higher spiritual kind.

If you turn towards the instincts of the higher spiritual species, it is possible that you can learn to master your emotions instead of letting them master you (see Pyramid 10 for help to work with your emotions). This is where you communicate when you leave the body on your astral travels during the day and dreamtime. The Etheric and Physical bodies then remain on Earth; during dreamtime you leave these two bodies in bed.

Layer 2. The Etheric Body: This body is closest to your Physical body and is the mold for it. It is the last layer before physical mass arises. As you can imagine, the energy frequencies here are quite close to your physical level, and you can easily perceive them. When you do this, you say that they are "on a higher level," because you cannot see them with your physical eyes. It is the energies here that are used in treatment and diagnosis of energy blockages. Your senses and chakras, energy centers, are located in this body. The Etheric body works closely together with the Physical body, and the two can be regarded as one.

Layer 1. The Physical Body: Your Physical body is the body you know as the person you are. The Physical body consists of the four elements (earth, fire, water, and air) and creates solid form, that is your mass. The fifth element (metal or ether; there are different names for this element) is connected to your thoughts. If you look upon this explanation, you will understand that you are so much more than your Physical body. The physical shell is something that you have to carry in order to dwell and act on the third density level.

This was a very brief explanation, but what I would like to point out is that you should know these twelve layers if you work with healing and energy work. When you work with another person, you should imagine these twelve layers, which you then go through layer by layer to purify and heal. This work I call lightwork, and it is explained in Part 3.

The Twelve Chakras of the Human Body

The task of the chakra system and the elements is to maintain the energy system of the physical body. Together they also maintain the meridian system and gather energy both from above and below. They also create the pulses that prevent blockages and diseases from being created in your bodies. They create the person you are by influencing you and your personality. They cooperate on many levels, both inside and outside of the body. They constitute a link for exchange, transmission, and communication. Transmissions mostly deal with energy.

Your chakras are created via the twelve sacred rays from Prime Creator. Within the physical body there are seven main chakras, and outside the body there are five more. Several smaller chakras also exist. A chakra is a kind of energy center, an energy wheel or vortex. The chakra system belongs to the etheric body. A chakra is a transformer of high frequency energy, which is distributed down into manageable energy in the physical body. The chakras transform the energy down through the layers of the twelve bodies into a pillar of light in the physical body. From the pillar, the energy is then distributed to your body through the meridians. Each chakra produces a color, in accordance with the frequency of the chakra, and the chakras all have their specific properties and affect each other.

The chakras are connected with the etheric pyramids and the planetary bodies in the Milky Way and the respective Universe. If one chakra gets out of balance, the energy flow to the body is reduced. At the same time, the other chakras are then affected, and this can lead to physical discomfort and disease.

In order to influence chakras that have been blocked, you can work with yoga, visualization exercises, meditations, Qi Gong, breathing exercises, and healing work. Light and sound work is very effective, i.e., to bring in light or sound to increase the movement, the energy of the chakra. The sounds can be introduced through a drum or through singing. In the course of the work, you can open your chakras like swinging doors that are opened inward into your twelve layers.

A lot of things are going on right now in your chakras. Firstly, you are releasing all the blockages within you, but you are also centering yourself. You interconnect your upper and lower chakras. You will all sense different chakra areas and feel how they merge to unite in the heart.

There are simply preparations going on for opening, purification, cleansing, and merging. Try to consciously have the intention to bring your lower and higher chakras together. This will cause you to eventually create three inner chakras. Those outside the body will remain as they are, but the seven inside will turn into three. There is a connection with the Trinity. In order to start the flows and to unite the lower and higher chakras in the heart, feel that your chakras are beginning to flow out, take a new form, and meet. It sounds more complicated than what it is. It is so simple, because everything you have worked with for a long time outside your body is now going to be centered inside the body.

The Base/Root Chakra is situated beside the genitals and communicates with the Earth. This chakra stimulates the gonads, the testes and the ovaries. A good contact with your root chakra helps you feel grounded and safe and deals with your inner power, strength, and centering. The root is associated with the physical and material aspects in life. The chakra color here is red, and this chakra is connected to the element earth.

The Sacral/Sexual Chakra is located slightly below the navel. This chakra creates the color orange and stimulates the pelvis, the legs, and the feet. It is closely related to your sexuality and self-control. To prevent this area from getting out of balance, it is important to love oneself and to not be in need of acknowledgment from others. Here many emotions like joy, passion, and anger arise.

The Solar Plexus Chakra is situated in the diaphragm. It produces the color yellow and is in connection with the element fire. In order not to have imbalance here, you have to believe in yourself, trust that everything that happens is correct. Here your fears are created, but also the genuine true feeling, which is love. If you have an open Solar Plexus Chakra, you also have a good contact with your emotions.

The Heart Chakra is located in the middle of the sternum. It produces the color green or pink and is connected to the element air. Here both joy and sadness are created. Here is given the opportunity to experience genuine and true forgiveness and to feel unconditional love for yourself and others. If you feel consideration for yourself and others, this area will keep its energy. The foundation for this is love of yourself. If you are in the Heart Chakra, you are centering your energy here and can open up for powerful healing, healing on all levels, both for yourself, other people, animals, and Mother Earth.

The Throat Chakra is situated behind the suprasternal fossa and is connected to the element air. This chakra creates the ability to express yourself, receive, and to speak out. This is the chakra for all kinds of communication. An open Throat Chakra gives you the ability to communicate with people, to be understood, and to understand others. If you have blockages here, you will find it difficult to make decisions. The color created here is blue.

The Forehead/Third Eye Chakra is located behind the middle of the forehead. The color here is indigo. This chakra connects you with your intuition. To keep the energy flowing here, you must have confidence in yourself, your inner knowledge, and intuition. Blockages here make people leave the main road and wander off on side paths. In those cases, you forget the meaning of life, the plan you yourself established before entry into the physical body. An open Forehead Chakra creates psychic abilities and provides the opportunity for higher communication.

The Crown Chakra is situated atop the crown of your head and includes the purple color or the divine white color. This chakra is closely connected with your spirituality. An open Crown Chakra provides opportunity for higher communication, guidance, and healing. This chakra is in communication with all the other chakras. This chakra gives you the ability to walk the right ways that lead you forward in life.

Chakras 8 and 9 are located both above your crown and below your feet. Here unperceivable breaking colors are created that originate from the refraction of the light in the prism. We can call these chakras receivers that receive and transform information that is then passed on through the Crown Chakra to the physical body and the brain. The information comes both from above and from Gaia, the Earth. Chakra 9 balances and holds together the body using polarity and magnetism, among other things.

The 10th Chakra is situated in your hands and under your feet, and it stands for the connection between Heaven and Earth. Every time you download frequencies from the Universe to do healing work, you work with the 10th Chakra. Every time you hear a tone or consciously ground yourself, you work with frequencies from this chakra.

Chakras 11 and 12 rotate along a circular line around your body. These chakras cooperate with the other chakras and hold all their information. Here the twelve sacred rays are transformed, to be restructured and create the other chakras. Outside these chakras are the twelve bodies that the chakras create links to for exchange of information between them.

The 11th Chakra is in close communication with the layers of the Metapersal body and contains the patterns that all the chakras carry. If you take all the chakras and pack them together into a little seed, then you have the 11th Chakra.

The 12th Chakra is very subtle and contains the pattern to create all the chakras. It is in communication with the twelfth sacred ray, which includes all frequencies and has connection to the soul.

The Elements of the Human Body

Just like the Earth, you have elements in your physical body that are sustained by energies from the sacred rays from Prime Creator. The elements also have a strong connection to the energy of the Earth, and they are also maintained by it.

There are five elements in the physical body. The elements go by different names in different civilizations. I have chosen here to use those names that are most common and which you recognize. You can actually call them whatever you want, but it is the names that are used within Eastern philosophy that I use here.

Your Physical body is maintained by **the element earth.** On many occasions I have spoken about the importance of being in between— finding balance through purification and cleansing so that you can be as grounded as you are connected to Prime Creator, to be in the middle.

It is important that you find the element earth inside the base of your body and gain understanding of the power of the element from Prime Creator. Just as you should stand balanced between Heaven and Earth, it is now time to start balancing your body inside. Do you understand the difference?

It is time to center the knowledge so that you prepare your physical body for the increase in frequency that will happen on Earth. The Earth is strongly associated with your base. In the base there is a power, an energy that is strengthened by the rays I have talked about. It is time to awaken this power, the kundalini energy. It now lies vibrating inside your base and spinal cord. By becoming aware of the elements in your physical body, you will bring the kundalini power to life. Let this energy awake. But you should, of course, not ask for the power to explode inside you, and such a thing will not happen. Just go inside yourself and ask for those energies to start moving. This is something that has already happened completely automatically in many of you who have testified about back ache and back pain.

The releasing of the kundalini energy must be done in several steps, so that you do not let loose the power and it starts rising too quickly to your head. When it reaches your brain and your physical memory, you will simultaneously learn to master the element fire. The divine fire will pulsate through all the cells in your entire body.

You must now actively go in with your intention, your desire to let this power awaken. From now (May 2012) on, the power will get started, and then it will slowly rise inside of you. It is in the meditative state, when you visit the Lemurian frequencies in Pyramid 5, that you will awaken the kundalini power. The body is ready to start the flow with the upcoming raisings of frequency on Earth at hand. But it will not happen overnight. It will take the necessary time and take place at a pace you can cope with. Remember that with every day that goes by, you rise in frequency, just like the Earth.

I have previously received questions about the symbol of medicine, the symbol with the two snakes winding around a staff. The snakes symbolize the kundalini, the holy river of God, which shall awake. It stretches like tubes or snakes, from the base of your body all the way up to your head. This is the secret behind this symbol. The fifth pyramid, the Lemurian, will help you to awaken it. It will happen completely automatically, but you must include in your intention that it is time to awaken the power. It is now, in this time, that it is time for the kundalini to awaken. Just relax and let your own body do the work for you, together with your guides.

We continue to **the Etheric body,** which receives its energy and exchanges power with the sacred cosmic fire, **the element fire.** It is of great importance that the cosmic fire gets to flow freely in your bodies, which it does if you can connect the element fire with the kundalini energy that flows out from the root chakra. When the cosmic fire enters your heart, you can put your focus there and center the energies there. This is in order for you to consciously be in your heart, instead of in your mind. When you are in your heart with the intention that your heart is going to open and that you are going to live and think lovingly, then the divine fire will automatically flow in your bodies and help the kundalini energy to start flowing freely. The energy flows and the fire are maintained in the body through your breathing.

The Emotional body gets energy from and is supported by **the element water.** The Throat and Solar Plexus areas are power sources for this element. The emotional body drives the motion of energies in your physical body. This motion will be developed fully when you connect with the kundalini energy from the root chakra.

The element water has a direct connection both to the root chakra, just like the other elements, and also to the heart. It is time to unite the divine with the earthly inside your physical body. This means that when you focus and center yourself inside your heart and get help to master the four main elements, you will also be able to reconcile lower and higher chakras with each other and in this way also ease the transition. You will find the hidden keys to higher knowledge about how you are going to transcend into a higher frequency.

The energies in **the Mental body** are maintained by **the element air.** That is why I speak about the importance of breathing the right way. If you breathe right, the energy will flow in the right direction inside your physical body. Your breathing is affected by the divine main breathing, the great inhalation and exhalation that go straight into you. Unfortunately, many of you inhibit this breathing and do not let it flow freely in the body. This prevents the energies from moving like they should in your energy pathways. This causes you to create stagnation and eventually disease.

You have reached so far in your purification process that you only need to focus on how to work with the flows of the energies inside your bodies, center the higher and lower chakras in the heart, and get the kundalini energies going, so that they are awakened and the snakes start winding around inside your bodies.

All power sources have a direct connection with the inner physical body and its chakra areas. You do not have to know the details, but only that it is time to start mastering the elements and get your energies flowing. When you start mastering the elements and get the kundalini energies to rise up to your head, you will also be able to balance your hemispheres. Then you will take command over the energies that the brain sends out twenty-four hours a day throughout your existence.

When you take command over these frequencies, you will also be able to put yourself into a particular state of mind whenever you like. Any time during the day, you will be able to increase or decrease any of the brain waves, depending on what your physical body needs right then. This gives you a glimpse of what the Lemurians did in conjunction with their raising. When you get the brain in balance, the energies of your physical body will also automatically be in balance. Everything is interconnected.

The Chakras, Elements, and Energy Grid of the Earth

The exact positions of the Earth's chakra areas are about to change. You will soon get to know how the system is built, through your own inner knowledge. You can actually ignore the positions, even though I mention some of them here briefly. Here are where some of the chakras of the Earth are located:

Δ Mount Shasta, a mountain in California in western USA,
Δ Lake Titicaca in South America,
Δ The sacred mountain in Uluru-Kata Tjuta in Australia,
Δ Glastonbury-Shaftesbury in England,
Δ The Pyramid of Cheops in Egypt
Δ Mount Kailash, a sacred mountain in Tibet

The Earth's Forehead Chakra or Third Eye has constantly been moving, based on the position of the zodiac in the firmament. The chakra is right now (in April 2012) positioned over Iran, and this creates turbulence, as you have noticed. The humans there are far from the time of enlightenment. It lies in their genetic heritage; they are guardians of the first tale of mankind and the cradle of civilization. It is not a coincidence that this chakra is situated exactly there, right now. I wish that you, via your forehead chakras, meditate and send energy to this country and its neighbors, to heal and to help decrease the turbulence.

There are five more chakras, but I choose to talk about the one that exists in Sweden. You call this place the Siljan Ring, and it is distinguishable from high above. You can connect directly there and get access to all the information, healing, and curing from all other chakra areas.

You have enlightened yourself to a higher level and have risen in frequency, which means that through the eleventh chakra you have access to all the chakras of the Earth. In the eleventh chakra, the patterns of all other chakras are gathered. Try in meditation to connect to this

70

chakra. Then you will heal yourself and thereby also the systems of the entire planet. When the Earth, which is a macrocosm, is healed, then the inhabitants of the planet are also healed. The purpose of the Earth's chakra areas is, of course, to heal and to lead energy to your Earth.

In order to access the highest ability, you must, of course, open all the keys in the Pyramid Matrix (see Part 4) and work with the frequencies there. There are twelve main chakras, but also many small ones. In addition to the chakra systems, there are smaller vortexes that build, create, and hold together the five elements.

The vortex for the element earth is located over Table Mountain in South Africa. The vortexes for the other elements are located as follows: the element water in New Zealand, the element air at the Pyramid of Cheops in Egypt, and the element fire in Hawaii. The vortex for the often-forgotten element metal is located over Beijing in China.

The body (Paula) had a mission in January 2012. She thought that she was going on vacation to South Africa, but she had a job to do. She was given the task to go up on Table Mountain and go into deep meditation, into a trance state. She completed the task and remembers that she met many spiritual co-workers who followed her via the vortex of the element earth down and into Mother Earth. She worked for exactly 42 minutes, and afterwards she was dizzy and experienced that a pulse, a kind of heartbeat, was started. She felt pulses under her feet on the entire mountain and in the earth. The pulses spread. Her task was to turn this spiral or vortex in the opposite direction. She simply restarted the Earth's chakra system and the Earth's five elements by turning the vortex in the opposite direction. This happened on the third day of the new year. I mention this because the pulses that were started on Table Mountain have now reached the Nordic countries. They are slowly spreading all across the world.

Start going out into woods and fields, and you will feel the pulsations that the body (Paula) started. When she started the energy vortex in the opposite direction, the entire clock got started. The clock or wheel that I speak about consists of the Matrix of the twelve etheric pyramids (see Part 4). It is these twelve pyramids that hold together the great grid of energy pathways that crisscross all over the world. You will learn to sense, perceive, and use these for refilling of energy and for teleporting yourself. The strongest energy is in Egypt, at the Pyramid of Cheops, the heart of the Earth.

Humanity has built sacred places, both on the chakra areas that I have mentioned and also on these energy pathways, which you call meridians, that run all over the Earth. On every meridian there are many sacred buildings, sacred temples, churches, and physical pyramids, and also sacred mountains and other natural formations. All over the Earth, the Matrix is maintained by means of physical buildings that send out energy to the grid. In addition to these buildings on the meridian lines, there are many sacred buildings and stone statues placed on the grids that are created by Curry-, Hartmann- and Ley-lines across the Earth. The energies of these lines also participate in maintaining the energy of the Matrix.

All the sacred places around the world, which many of you have visited, are involved in building and maintaining the Matrix, the grid that surrounds the Earth and protects the Earth and the process of creation. When we open by using the keys, it is important that as many as possible within a certain time rise in frequency into the new Golden Age. This has to happen. That is why many of you feel the fear of a pole shift which you fear might happen. Troubled times weaken the energy and the magnetism around the planet. If you rise in frequency, you never need to worry that the planet will perish. It is just to keep up with it.

So now I encourage all of you to go out and feel the pulses in the woods and connect to the pulse of the Earth. When you do this, start playing, be joyous, and feel happiness in your bodies. There are so many that are so sad, in all the groups that I meet. Your hearts are closed then, my friends. If you are to open your heart, then bring forth the playfulness inside you, start living in your heart.

From the moment you wake up tomorrow morning, try to feel happiness for a new day, that you open your eyes and get to be a part of the fantastic things happening on Earth around you. Feel the tingling in your body like in a little child on Christmas Eve before it is time for the Christmas gifts. Expectation, happiness. Try to foster this feeling every morning when you wake up. If you do this, the feeling will spread more and more during the day. For each moment you feel happiness and expectation, you will open up a little bit more. Then you slowly will take command over your physical body and demand your unconscious self to step aside. Thereafter, wish instead to get in contact with your Higher Self.

The Twelve Sacred Rays

The twelve sacred rays start from Prime Creator and affect you strongly, just as the frequencies from the twelve pyramids do. The rays are sacred, and each ray includes an attribute, a knowledge. The twelve rays pass through all of the twelve pyramids. There are facts to read about these rays and people who teach about them. The problem is that the books and the teaching do not include the last five rays.

You must become aware that everything has twelve frequency layers. Man has from time immemorial talked about seven cosmic rays, because you have seven chakras in your physical bodies. This I want to explain and clarify. Of course, there are twelve rays, my friends, and not seven. All of the rays contain the seven chakra colors, plus five other colors that cannot be perceived and seen on this physical plane. There are twelve rays, and some of them make themselves stronger felt during certain months. This has to do with the year and the zodiac. You are all connected to all the rays, but you have a stronger connection to one or some of them.

The zodiac of astrology, which consists of twelve signs, affects the power of these rays. Man is affected and becomes influenced by the rays at the moment of birth. One is, so to speak, born through a pyramid, a power, and a ray. All of the rays illuminate Earth continuously, but sometimes stronger or weaker, depending on how the Earth is in the constellation relative to the rest of the Cosmos. This means that you, depending on your moment of birth, attract more or less of the attributes of certain rays. All of the rays overlap, and you can have stronger attraction to several of these rays. Nine of the rays are attribute rays that support the three primary rays.

The first primary ray is about the driving force in man, your story of creation, your ability to understand the meaning of evolution, and your ability to will. It is also about power and the ability to perform planned tasks, to act—not just think.

The second primary ray is about love. Love for family, oneself, and so on. If you have a problem nurturing love for some people, then you are not in line with this ray.

The third primary ray is about higher knowledge, the ability to open up and receive higher knowledge. We are not talking about science, but about higher esoteric knowledge. This knowledge is interesting, because there can be no higher knowledge if the two other primary rays are not incorporated. Everything is interconnected.

You do not achieve wisdom until you stop adapting yourself and instead follow your heart. When new information, that you feel is right for you, reaches into your heart and you start living according to this new knowledge, then you have reached wisdom, my friends. By positively and correctly adjusting yourself according to this new knowledge that you feel is right in your heart, you will achieve wisdom. It does not matter how many books you read, how many courses you take, how many fathers and mothers who give you lectures; if it is not taken into the heart, you can never achieve wisdom, only unfounded knowledge.

The fourth ray is about creativity, artistry, and development of the ability to think in new ways. To not only use the logical mathematical part of the brain but start to use new ways of thinking. To develop creative thinking and the realization of dreams and thoughts. This does not only apply to art, music, or literature, but to actually creating through energy and your thoughts. Creating can occur on many different planes and levels.

The fifth ray is about concrete knowledge, that which you call science. Some people always need a scientific explanation.

The sixth ray is about dedication, the ability to follow a belief, a religion, or higher teachings. It is about your belief of what is right and wrong in society, and confidence in laws and regulations. Many people are righteous and maybe at the most drive their car a little too fast. You understand that this ray has had a strong impact in your lives. Do you let your inner belief come through? I do not speak about religion. If you do not follow your inner belief and inner wisdom, but go against it, then you will lose contact with your Higher Self. This is exactly what happens when you adapt yourself; you go against yourself (see the eighth ray).

The seventh ray is about your organizational ability. If you are disorganized, you do not have that much contact with this ray.

The eighth ray is about your ability to adapt, both the positive and the negative when it comes to your adaptability. Here it is about being able to adapt oneself without losing one's inner conviction or creating negative emotions.

The ninth ray is about fears and the ability to let go and receive. Daring to take leaps in life and reach the goals that you have set. Learning to solve problems and overcome obstacles to emerge stronger from different situations.

The tenth ray is about the personality, your patterns. The personality, merged from all planes and existences, the form you have been molded into as a result of all your earlier incarnations.

The eleventh ray is about your ability to live according to the knowledge and the lessons that you receive during life and connect this with all that you have inside of you from all your earlier existences. This ray includes all knowledge from all rays.

The twelfth ray includes the totality of all the other rays and frequencies from Prime Creator. It is the soul's connection down to the Mother (the Earth) and to the Father (Prime Creator). It is a direct link between Prime Creator and your soul. It is the link between your Higher Self and your subconscious. It creates balance, a harmony that means centering, to be in the middle between Heaven and Earth.

When you enter a pyramid, you do not need to know which ray, planet, or body sends down its frequency and where the frequencies enter and affect you. Just feel how you open up your power to receive. For the power to be stronger, you open up and receive your energy also from the planets. You do not need any names to get a connection; it happens automatically.

So stop thinking so much, my dears. You do not need to understand how everything works. Maybe someday I will choose to go deeper into this if I feel that you humans are in need of it. But when you enter a pyramid, it is sufficient to know that there is a ray from Prime Creator that goes straight into this pyramid. It partially affects its frequency, but it is unimportant to know exactly in what way.

Do you begin to understand that everything is connected? What did I say—life is easy to live. Begin each morning with a little shot of love for yourself. And decide not to give a single thought to what happened yesterday, because yesterday does not exist. There is only now, here and now, not yesterday and not tomorrow, but here and now. This way life becomes easy to live. Never adapt yourself to another individual again.

Examine yourself! Do you practice what you have been taught? Remember that you can never reach wisdom, you can never call yourself enlightened, as long as you do not practice what you learn and follow your heart.

The Planets

If we widen the perspective a little—I have told you that the cell is a copy of the Universe, that you are all linked with each other, with creation, and with the highest frequencies that you call God. You can imagine that from the tiniest cell in your body, threads of light go out, straight through your twelve bodies to the twelve pyramids and further up to their respective planet.

The twelve pyramids are in their respective frequencies and are connected higher up in the system. You call your system the Milky Way, and there are different planets with similar frequencies. Eventually we will connect these pyramids on a higher level in order to reach the respective planetary system with its frequency.

All planets continuously send out frequencies that reach your physical bodies all the way down on a cellular level. These are the frequencies, all the way from Prime Creator, that form the basis of all change on the planet. Among other things, they give rise to the beautiful patterns and formations on Earth that you call crop circles. These are direct images and patterns of the frequencies of the celestial bodies in the Milky Way. In your physical bodies these patterns are reflected all the way down to the lowest level of the atom, and they affect you physically, both how you feel and how you evolve. Your physical bodies consist of all elements that exist. Consequently, all patterns are within you, and you feel the patterns of the crop circles strongly when you see them in pictures or in real life.

Every planetary body has its orbit around the Sun, and the planets create sound/frequencies that create images/patterns. Mathematicians can make a drawing of them, and they are used in different contexts. I guess you all, during physics and chemistry classes in school, have built molecules, geometrical shapes with plus and minus charged poles. You can raise your frequencies through contact with these patterns to create a stronger vibration of these in your physical bodies. This creates a resonance in your physical bodies that strengthens the pattern in them.

The Universe consists of important numbers and patterns. One of these is the number twelve. Your planet is part of a planetary system with twelve planets and one sun, a total of thirteen bodies. You haven't discovered all the planets yet, because some of them vibrate with such a high frequency that you in your earthly frequency cannot perceive them. They have no physical mass, so your physical sun cannot illuminate them.

I would like to talk about your Milky Way. There are more celestial bodies in it than you and your scientists know about. However, I only have permission to talk about those that you already know of. I will not inform you about more than the position of the first pyramid in the solar system at this point. This because it affects and limits many of you in your upcoming work.

My work consists of sowing a seed in you so that you will understand who you are in relation to the Universe. To understand how things are constructed. You will gradually receive much more information about every planet. The power of the planets is enormous and affects the personalities of humans. Besides the Sun, there are, as recently mentioned, twelve planets in your planetary system. In addition, many moons and other smaller celestial bodies exist that also affect man. The influence of the planets on man varies, depending on their internal relationship and their positions in the zodiac.

The planetary positions in the zodiac at birth is of special importance. You all know that according to astrology, the planetary positions at the birth of a human being are what determine the life conditions, possibilities, and psyche of the newborn. Of course, the twelve sacred rays, our Universe, the twelve other Universes, Prime Creator, and my Matrix are also important factors for the life of the newborn.

Planet X is located in your system, but comes back at intervals of more than 3,000 years. It is now approaching. Right now it is located close to your Sun—that is, inside your solar system. You must not forget this celestial body in your upcoming work. That is why I begin with it. The frequency of this planet is very high, and that is the reason for the long orbit. It affects man. Planet X carries frequencies that affect your subconscious mind, your subconscious thoughts, and the encounter with your previous existences and old memories from previous existences. If you connect to the frequency of this planet, you can meet and process old memories in your bodies. It is directly linked to one of the twelve pyramids. Dare to let go of your ego.

The frequencies of **Mercury** are connected to the power of thought, the ability to change your thoughts, send out, receive, and change your frequencies. Your thought patterns have to change with the New Age approaching. The frequencies affect your communications and the ability to convey your thoughts. The frequencies from here also stimulate your hemispheres and logical thinking.

Start your day by giving thanks for a new beautiful day. Change your thought patterns from scratch for the transformation to take place in each of you.

Every day the frequencies are raised, and your thoughts become stronger and stronger when sent out. What you wish for rebounds back on each one of you. You have to believe in yourself, your power, and the magic you can create merely by your physical being.

It is time to send out pure thoughts. You cannot send pure thoughts to others if you do not first send pure thoughts to yourself. Think healthy thoughts to yourself each moment, every minute, dreamtime included. The first and greatest change and transformation that must happen is that you change all dark, destructive thoughts. You can only create this change through active work to change every dark and negative thought. Be present.

The Sun is an important celestial body and the life giver to all the twelve planets. It is the only one that I am allowed to connect to a pyramid, Pyramid 1. The Sun is the base, inner balance, and centering. Ancient civilizations worshiped the Sun god, and this was partly due to the connections with the frequencies from the Sun to Pyramid 1.

Work with the frequencies from inside out in your bodies. Here it is also about courage, optimism for the future, and inner desire. The frequencies from the Sun create your identity, vitality, and basic energy.

The frequencies of **the Earth and the Moon** open your heart and help you to let go. Here it is about the love for the Earth and for yourself. To love oneself is the foundation of all love. Through the frequencies of Earth you can reach spiritual awakening, cosmic wisdom, clarity of vision, and acceptance. You think that you carry a burden on your shoulders; learn to let go of this burden.

In the frequency of the Earth you find balance and focus, and automatically connect to trance and other meditative states. The Earth is closely related to the Moon, which also affects you strongly.

The frequency of the Moon affects your individual thought patterns, to distinguish you from others. If you have difficulties with this, you can connect to the frequency of the Moon to learn how to separate yourself from others. Learn to live without taking on others' frequencies/ burdens and pains. Life is not a bed of roses, but you live to learn and to face obstacles. The energy of the Moon affects the tides and stands for fertility and reproduction in man. The frequencies from the Moon affect your habits, behaviors, and unconscious attitudes.

Venus has a very beautiful pattern, which includes the feminine principles. Here it is about caretaking, the power to be able to live in joy, harmony, beauty, romance, humor, and also the social aspects. People who do not have good social skills can work with the frequencies of Venus. Very male-oriented principles can be balanced with this planet. Through these frequencies you learn to give and receive love and to mediate attraction.

Mars stands for the male principles, to set goals, and to work to succeed in reaching them. If you have problems focusing on your goals and completing them, you lack the frequencies from Mars and need to work with them. Many people have thoughts, but they never convert them into practical action; the frequencies calibrate incorrectly. Mars affects the physical capacity for writing and speech, to take in and convey knowledge. The frequencies from here also stand for strength, power, courage, aggression, sexuality, and the ability to assert and defend oneself.

Jupiter is a beautiful formation. Here the ability to take on guilt and pain is found. Disharmonious childhood and adolescence gives disharmonious individuals, due to external influences. The ability to not take on things and to let them flow off shows that you have a high frequency of Jupiter. If you had a tough adolescence, it is good to work a lot with the frequencies of Jupiter. Here also are found frequencies for inner growth, to heal suppressed emotions, belief, sense of justice, the pursuit of spiritual growth, and the search for individual meaning of life.

The frequencies of **Saturn** affect different emotions, the power of thought, and the fears that hinder your way forward. Saturn consists of much gas, and not much matter. The gas affects your frequencies in a positive way. When you work with your lifeline you often touch upon the frequency of Saturn, also when working with many of the other planets, but Saturn in particular. Here you find the frequencies for the ability to reach relaxation and concentration. Work with managing the duties that you need in order to operate in your everyday life and unnecessary musts. Find the balance between these two to find the most necessary ones. Here you also find the human sense of how to perceive reality, for morality, maturity, responsibility, and consequences.

Uranus. Many of your dreams exist here, both physical and astral. It is about fulfilling dreams, to see clearly. Many wander about on side paths and do not walk on the right road, their main road. This planet is about this. When you wander about on side paths, you might not catch your dream, but live someone else's. Fulfill your dream and your original plan, perhaps with the help of knowledge of a higher order, to prevent yourself from spending time on another similar life. In this frequency, you can work with jealousy and other addictions that prevent you from fulfilling your dreams. It is easy to wind up in addiction if you do not take care of yourself. The frequencies here are about having the courage to let go of one's limitations, get new ideas, and sudden inspiration, daring new things. The rebels on Earth have a strong connection to the frequencies of Uranus.

Neptune is about dreams, illusions, and the need to feel freedom and to be original, to stand out from the rest. Here you also find the domestic feelings that also exist in Venus' frequencies. Neptune helps with the feelings of affinity with the group, unselfish giving, and universal love. Through the frequencies of Neptune, you can reach higher dimensions, reach spiritual wisdom, and dissolve the ego. Changes that have to be made in life have their origins here. For example, changes in diet that are required with the New Age approaching.

Pluto is about "going home" and about transitions in life from child to youth, from woman to mother, student to employee, etc., but primarily about the journey home after this life on Earth. The cycle of dying and living. If you have trouble with transitions in life, then work a lot with the frequencies of Pluto. The frequencies here stimulate man to resolve old things and take in new things in life, to stand in one's full power throughout life, to be personal or not, to have control or to be helpless, and to deal with changes and transformations.

The Twin Planet/Tellus 2. This is a planet that is starting to become visible and which has no physical mass. It is called the twin of the Earth. It is located at the same distance from the Sun as the Earth, and it is slightly larger. This one is interesting. When you were children, you asked the question inside of you, "Surely it cannot only be me who is me; there must be somebody out there somewhere, right?" Science is funny in that it still is searching for alien life forms in the form of bacteria. If they only knew the life forms that exist. This planet influences in a similar way that the Earth does.

When you start to work with the frequencies of the pyramids, you will automatically receive more information about the planets. Their frequencies permeate the planets.

You will visit the planets in different orders, and you still don't know which planet is more linked to a certain pyramid. Remember that much of what I am talking about merges into each other. Some frequencies are very close to each other. Just open up for the opportunity to take in the frequency of each respective planet/celestial body as you meditate on the pyramids.

To connect with a planet, visualize that you will reach the right planet, see the planet in your mind's eye, and feel how a thread or the like goes out through the pyramid further up into the Milky Way to the right planet. Imagine that you work with its frequencies to strengthen or reduce the frequency in your body.

When you work with frequencies, you can also heal yourself. The twelve celestial bodies contain the frequencies of the twelve pyramids. Thus, the pyramids were created from the frequencies of the celestial bodies (descending transformation of light/sound).

There are twelve Universes that are constructed by the same principle, with similar frequency levels that include systems similar to your own. There are many galaxies which all are contained in a Universe.

Thoth's Advice to Us Now

So my advice to each one of you is this: *Begin every day by feeling happiness in your bodies and the pulse in nature.* Go out in nature and start communicating with everything you meet. All plants, trees, and animals. When you feel the pulse of nature, connect your energy with it. Start listening to your intuition every day, and let go of the forced imprints you carry as a result of your adaptation. Let go and follow all the desires of your heart. Stop walking around like robots, who hoard material things and live adapted to someone else's life. Understand that you are part of something big and sacred, that all humans, whether you know them or not, also are a part of you. I have said it before and I say it again: *Love yourself!*

Look upon all your fellow human beings as your equals. Understand that all have the same value. When you see a person lying in the street or on a park bench, then what do you do? Most people shut their eyes and hurry by. Instead, sit down next to the person, put a hand on their cheek, and tell the dropout that he or she is valuable and beautiful. Then send light and love to the person. By that, you show that all fellow human beings have the same value, no matter if one lies on a park bench or not. How do you think this person would react to your touch? These people are used to people whispering, pointing fingers, or rushing past them. This action would go straight into the heart.

What I want you to always carry with you is the moment when you took your firstborn baby in your arms and you looked down. The moment when you were fully in your heart, opened yourself, and felt only love. It is such a moment you should carry with you in your memories. A moment that shows exactly what it is like to be in the heart. Every time you wish to be in this state again, see the child and just feel how the love radiates. If you do not have a child, you can imagine that you carry a child or yourself as a child in your arms. It is a parable for you to understand how it feels to be in the heart. Can you imagine the feeling when nothing else exists around you, apart from this particular little creation?

You will be able to transform this feeling of your greatness that has created this very being, and you will understand that you are such a miracle. For each time you can keep this feeling in your body, time will feel like an eternity, a long time, as time does not exist linearly.

I have tried to give you a picture of what it is like to be in the heart. In order to heal and to cure on all levels, as many prophets and Masters have done at all times, the condition is to be in your heart. The ability to get there exists by following your intuition. When you listen to it and begin to follow your path, then bring along this question:

"What is my mission on Earth?"

Part 3

Healing Work

Thoth's Healing Lightwork

The New Age requires that many of you start to work with energy. Both by healing and curing yourselves, but also to help individuals in your surroundings who need support and help to move on in their transformation. It requires a different kind of work right at the beginning and the opening, so that you can receive the very highest frequencies. Take in these frequencies through your back, so that they will have the shortest possible way to cross through your physical body. Of course, this should happen only after you have opened your chakras.

Any physical disease has, at some point, been preceded by a thought from yourself, a thought that eventually resulted in a weakening of the body's barriers and protection mechanisms. In that way, the disease can penetrate your physical body.

What is energy and what is matter? Motion exists in both forms, even in that which you consider as solid matter. Denser energy gives more compact matter. If you fill this up with air, you can create vacuum and thereby increase the distance between the particles (i.e., decrease the density). You can start experimenting with energy on all planes. You are created from the energy of sound and light.

When you feel that you have lost contact with your main road and ended up on side paths, it would be a good idea that you heal yourself with healing work. Then you work with your intuition and contact with Prime Creator.

As I mentioned earlier, man's chakra system consists of twelve chakras. Outside of these is the body's energy field, that which you call the aura. The energy field is your twelve energy layers that constitute your bodies and consist of light and sound. Your energy field creates your physical body, which is made up of densified sound and light.

Many believe that it is the physical body that creates the energy field, but it is the other way around. Your physical body exists, thanks to your energy field, your aura. The physical body communicates constantly, every second, with your energy field. All the time, these two exchange experiences and knowledge through layer after layer, down to the smallest atom. The physical body acts, based on the information it gets from the energy field. All memories from all your existences are stored in this energy field.

The destructive and negative patterns (i.e., memories, imprints, and experiences) that are stored in the energy layers are reflected in the physical body and give rise to what you call disease. What happens to your physical body in this life, gives in turn an imprint in your energy layers and is stored there as patterns. Everything is stored in your energy layers and creates there your total memory bank. This is why you have to work with the energy around you when you are doing healing work.

You know that the body consists of cells, molecules, and atoms. These are exchanged in the body. A human being is renewed in full every seven years. If this happens, how is it that your diseases still remain? The patterns and the memories of your physical complaints remain in your light body, your energy field. Therefore, the healing work must also occur there.

Cleansing and Purifying

Step one. Start with your lifeline (see the next section) and purify and cleanse yourself as much as you can.

Step two is to cleanse and heal your own bodies through lightwork with the twelve layers, and later also by using Pyramid 2. Each one of you can feel well and become healthy. It sounds trite, but that is the case. Purify and cleanse your own energy fields, layer by layer, but remember that the unconscious messes things up for you. If you think that you are purified and cleansed, but have suppressed your feelings during your whole life, these may lie hidden from you. Therefore, it is important to receive help from others in the purification process.

Practice makes perfect, and you can become experts at spotting other people's suppressed emotional energies.

Change the focus of your healing work from just easing diseases and loosening blockages in the physical body (this is like taking medicine for treating symptoms) to also *removing the causes* in your energy field outside the physical body.

Step three. The basic principle of lightwork when you work with others is that you take in the light from Prime Creator through your back and straight into your heart area, which is the purest place in your body. By that, you minimize the risk that the energy is affected by your own energy and that which you yourself are carrying. Consequently, the energy from Prime Creator should take the shortest way with the least influence from you, in order to be kept as pure and untouched as possible. You will always affect the energy anyway, to a certain extent, but this method minimizes this influence. You do not need to use your hands, but you can send the energy straight out from your heart.

You can heal anything that comes your way: individuals, other living beings, places, and also the Earth. When you heal someone, you should pass through all the twelve layers. You send energy in via your open heart (see Exercise 1), layer by layer. Put effort and energy into your intention to bring in light and love from Prime Creator.

When you reach the last layer, the physical body, bring in the light through the head of the person, onwards down through the body, and out through the feet. The energy should then flow straight through the body without obstacles, since you already have worked in all the outer layers. If you face a blockage or obstacle inside the physical body, you will have to go back out in the outer layers and start from the beginning.

It is important that destructive and negative memories are erased and replaced by the information that the body is renewed and whole. Your intention here is of utmost importance. Bring in the pure light from Prime Creator through the twelve layers. The light will push out the dark from the person's energy field, if it is your intention for this to happen.

The energy body was transformed down when you left the drop in your descension to Earth. The outermost Atmic layer is directly linked to Prime Creator, Mother Earth, and your soul. In the outer layer of the Metapersal body is the fabric of that which will become the perfect energy of origin for each individual. In the layers of the Metapersal body, all frequencies from the twelve pyramids, the thirty-six sacred frequencies, are stored. These cooperate, and together with other frequencies, they create the knowledge you have with you and the physical body you are in.

Each one of you is closer to one of the pyramids. At the moment of birth, you were created through some of the frequencies, together with the sacred ray from Prime Creator. You can look upon the pyramids as an opportunity to work on all planes, all levels, to heal yourself and your physical body.

If you suffer from feelings that blind you or if you suffer from lack of patience, you can use the power of the pyramids to replenish, get answers, and to change. Never become blocked because of the texts that are recorded about the pyramids. Instead, raise your consciousness and notice that you can create everything you want through this system. Use your power and creativity to reach the keys on all planes and levels (The lightwork in its entirety, see Exercise 3 below).

The Line—
Let Go of Imprints, Fears, and Traumas

The Line is a technique that you can use to purify and cleanse yourself from imprints, fears, traumas, and other memories that obstruct your road right now.

In order to purify and cleanse your physical, mental, and emotional bodies, there are various techniques to use. The Line is a very simple and effective technique. It is important that you daily bring yourself into a meditative state where your brainwaves go down to Alpha level or even Theta level. In a meditative state, you can then work with your lifeline.

You need paper, pen, and peace and quiet. Start by drawing a line on a piece of paper. Mark on the line all the years you have lived on Earth: zero, one, two, three, four, five, six, and so on, up to your present age. You can even make a line for all your previous incarnations. Take another sheet of paper and write zero, one, two, three, four, five, and so on backwards for the lives you have lived. If you wish, you can then also make a similar sheet for all your future incarnations.

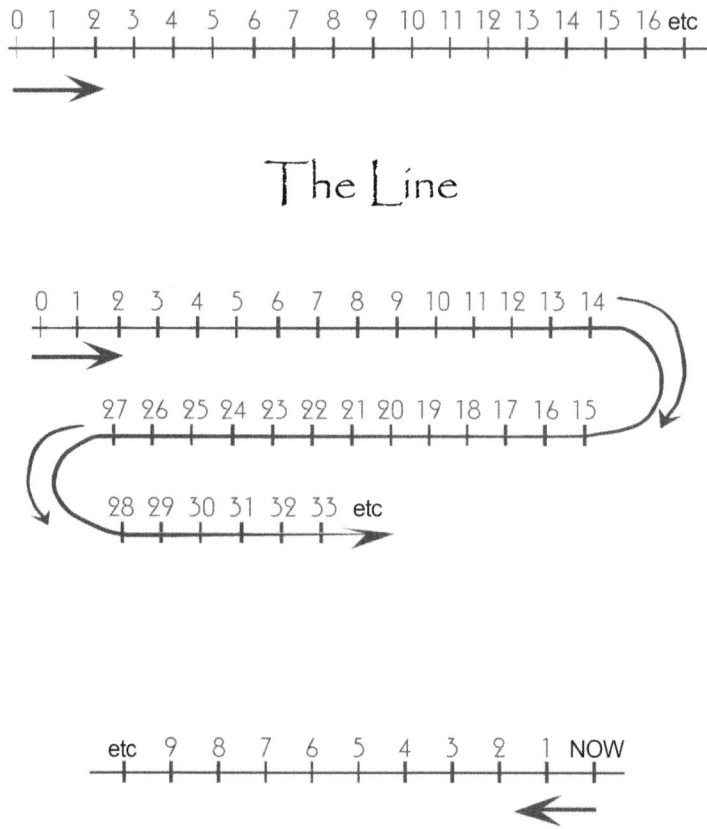

The Line

Follow the timeline and meditate on it. Follow the line and mark with a cross on it when you feel something in your bodies. Sometimes you perceive a feeling and sometimes memories. Sometimes you do not feel anything, but the work itself helps you to let go. You might experience warmth, a vibration, an impulse, coldness, heat, discomfort, or other similar feelings that touch you. Make cross markings on these occasions and then go back to work with each cross. Continue with cross after cross.

Many feelings may arise when you go through this process, and it can lead to many tears, but this will help you to be able to enter the pyramid of emotions (number 10) and reach the true and genuine Love when its key opens up within you. Then do the same with your past lives, from the present life and backwards. Forgiveness might often be required, both to yourself and sometimes to others.

The earlier a trauma arises, the fewer memories it will create. This is because of small children having defense mechanisms that embed and suppress unpleasant experiences in order to simply be able to survive. Small traumas can be enormous for small children and may create blockages in energy flows that follow them all the way up to adulthood. These traumas can be so small that you as adults cannot believe that they may have been an issue. With this line, you can bring forth that which obstructs you on your road through life and release your blockages, no matter if you are aware of them or not.

Work with every cross—and I promise you that there may be many of them on this sheet of paper. Try to reawaken the feeling that every cross gave rise to, even if you cannot remember the event. Sometimes you have to dive deeper into the feeling, scrutinize it, or relive the event. Ask that you never again will need to become obstructed or feel the pain that the event/feeling that you are throwing away has caused you.

After that, it is about letting go. Forgive yourself for carrying this within you for such a long time. Sometimes you should also forgive someone who has been co-creator of the trauma. If you want to, you can write down what comes to you. It can help you to let go. Then burn the paper, and feel that it leaves your physical body on all levels. Fill the void that arises with light and love, which you can collect from Pyramid 1 (see Part 4). Just enter the Crystal Room there and fill yourself with the healing tones and the light from Prime Creator.

You were all born into this particular incarnation because you have a work, an important work for your evolution, which has to be completed. It is not a coincidence that so many people are on Earth at this particular time when the New Age starts.

There are three steps to use to let go of imprints, fears, or anything that has gotten stuck and is blocking you.

△ You can just accept the event/feeling when you see that it exists, and then you let go of it.

△ Or you may have to dig deeper and bring forth the feeling and feel it. Try to perceive the whole situation, to then let go of it.

△ Or you may also have to go into yourself and forgive yourself and those around you for having put you in that situation.

You have to perform the processing at different depths, depending on how early in life the blockage was created or how difficult the situation was. The earlier the blockage was created, the harder the processing will be. I recommend that you perform this work to open your channels, so that your guides and counselors will get a clearer communication.

When you cleanse and purify blockages from previous incarnations, many of you will notice that you will put many crosses on the line between the lives and not just on a past life. To cleanse these blockages, whether they originate from previous incarnations or from sections between the lives, you can be greatly assisted by Pyramid 2 (see Part 4).

A lot of things can happen between lives. You can, for example, leave a traumatic earthly life, where you were subjected to violations of different kinds before you had trust in grown ups. You then leave that life to go through a purification, but you get stuck in the purification process. Instead of bringing these lessons to raise yourself and your frequencies to a new level and a new lesson, you choose to lower yourself and go down a couple of frequency levels. You choose to drop because you have been in earthly form for so long, during so many lives, and are attached to the traumas you have created on Earth during these existences.

You may have difficulties moving on and completing the mission that the traumatic life has created conditions for. Maybe the experiences could have led to you becoming a master, a teacher for others, or something similar. For a long time (although remember that time does not exist) you are stuck and do not respond to your higher helpers and close ones, who try to help you come out of this purification process that you got stuck in. Instead, it is possible that you eventually choose a new life, a new existence, and there recreate your traumas, because they are what you feel comfortable with.

This was a tragic example, but it happens very often that you simply cannot cope with the purification process. It may also be the case that you, on your way, when leaving a life upon Earth, are so strongly attached to one or more in that life that you do not cross over. You simply choose to stay and follow your near and dear ones until they also leave the earthly life.

There are many examples of what happens between lives. For example, it may be the case that you do not find your way home, but end up on the wrong level and must be helped to get home. There can be a variety of reasons for this. One is when you choose to end your life too early. It may also happen when the body is too infected by toxins or when you do not believe that any life exists after this and get in a drastic accident. In such situations it may happen that you are not led home properly. Then it may take time, but sooner or later you will all get where you should be. However, many of you have such a high consciousness level that this will not apply to you.

We can never force anyone who is shut down to get home. We can never change anyone's basic ideas. All we can do is to appear, and then the majority will follow the light home. But there are people who deny this light and refuse to follow.

During the purification process, one could say that you enter a spin-dryer that purifies you from less positive things to then rise up fully and leave the physical and inert matter completely. In a somewhat similar way, that will happen when Earth ascends into the fifth dimension, and you at times want to rise up into higher frequencies. You undergo a purification process.

Exercise 1
Opening your Heart and Concentrating the Energy

Opening your heart from the outside in helps you to protect it from energy and to not leak out your own energy. The heart is then also filled with the power of the Universe. Always assume that you bring in the energy from Prime Creator. Not from any other lower place.

Close your eyes and start to fill yourself from above with energy from Prime Creator, the light and sound. The fundamental tones fill your head and flow down like water in your body. When the energy reaches your feet, you let parts of it flow on down to Mother Earth.

Now imagine that a door is opened in your back. The energy now flows in from behind and into your heart. Your entire chest is filled with energy, both from the front and from behind.

Slowly draw together the energy from your feet and from your head to your heart area. This energy is now able to communicate with you, your soul and your subconscious mind. Let the communication give you answers on how you can live in your heart, love yourself, and forgive yourself for all the limitations that you have given yourself in life after life. Concentrate the energy and feel how it fills up your entire chest and heart. Do not belittle what comes to you.

Now feel how you distribute the energy back up into your head and down into your feet, and let it remain in your body. Close the door in your back. Also close the crown chakra from new flow.

Try to do this exercise every morning, where you fill yourself with energy, open up in your back, and concentrate the energy in your heart for a few moments. Also try to communicate with the energy. The power of thought is enormous.

At the same time, affirm to yourself what a fantastic individual you are. See your possibilities instead of your difficulties. Be grateful for every moment you have the possibility to be in physical form. Make the most of every moment you have here on Earth.

You can never love someone else if you do not love yourself from the depths of your heart. When you open up your heart more and more, you will also access the power that love brings. How do you think Jesus worked with healing energy while he was on Earth? There is no possibility that you can fully heal and cure others if you are not cured and healed yourself. Otherwise there is a risk that the energy you work with and send out is your own imprints, feelings, and thoughts.

The gifted healers who have served on Earth have all worked solely from their hearts. Remember to always turn off the power after the work is done, so that the energy of the heart is maintained and not emptied. Never use your basic energy, but only the energy you fill yourself up with from Prime Creator. Always fill up with the healing and purifying light from Prime Creator. Only the highest and purest energy.

Exercise 2
Raising Frequencies

Δ Relax and lean back in your chair. Drop your shoulders. Breathe deeply, feel how the air goes down through your trunk, down to your stomach. Feel how the breathing increases the vitality in your body.

Δ You will take in the energies from your back instead of from above. The energy goes from behind, straight into your heart area. Imagine how you open up a door in your back.

Ask Thoth to help you bring in powerful energy.

Δ Feel that your heart is opened. Not like you have done before, but in depth. Feel how your heart has the ability to pump out and distribute the energy upwards and downwards in your body, all the way down to your feet and up to the top of your crown.

Ask Thoth for help to activate healing energies and frequencies in your aura on a deeper level than what you have previously used.

Δ Feel how it flows in from all parts of your interior. Feel how heat spreads to your hands and also to your feet. By every step, you now heal the Earth and the ground you walk on. Now gather all the power around your heart.

Feel how the taps are opened.

Δ You are right now about to increase the frequency level in your physical body one level, to be able to receive even more energy from the Universe.

Behind you is a light being, who now puts his hands on you.

Δ Feel how your body is warmed up. The creational force is enormous, and miracles will be able to happen around you. The more healed your physical body gets, the greater miracles you can perform.

Now just relax and sit in the energies.

Exercise 3
Thoth's Lightwork

Practice this technique until it feels easy and simple, until it feels totally automatic and natural. When you work with healing, it is important to download the right frequency form. This is the first thing that you have to learn; miracles cannot happen if you do not use the right frequency form.

1. **Opening ceremony**

   Create a personal opening ceremony, where you ask for energy from Prime Creator, preferably via the Holy Trinity. By creating an opening, you also create a pattern that makes it easier and faster to connect to the energy of Prime Creator. A thought will suffice.

2. **Preparing to download the right frequency level and work from the Trinity**

   Open up the crown chakra—allow light, love, and energy to flow. The intention is the most important thing of the entire work. Calm your mind, ask what you can help with, and determine what is to be achieved with the work. Fill your body with sacred white light from Prime Creator, fill yourself with the Primal Force.

   Please repeat the following or something else that for you raises the intention and power in your work: *In the light of the Holy Trinity, I use the Highest Ones' Sacred frequencies from Prime Creator in my Lightwork.*

3. **The work**

   Δ Place yourself at the border between the person's aura and the atmosphere. Everything should be done from your heart—turn off your brain, and experience everything with your heart. No hands need to be used, only through your heart can you send out the sacred light energy with the power of thought. Do not cross any arms or legs, and stand up to be in contact with the Earth. Always start from your heart's power with the feeling of love. Without love, no healing and miracles can happen.

Δ Start by measuring/feeling where the outer border of the person's energy field is. Open up portals under your feet, draw up the power from Mother Earth, and fill up your entire body with the energy of Mother.

Δ Now again, draw down the sacred energy from Prime Creator through your crown chakra and fill your entire body. When your body is filled with both forms of energy, gather them together with all your power to your heart.

Δ Remember the exercise where you bring in the power through your back into your heart. That exercise makes it easy to gather the power in the heart area. Now step out of your body energetically and stand in front of yourself and look at yourself. Now open the swinging door straight in to your heart—the door goes inward, always inward, into the depths of your body and the area around your heart. Step through the door into yourself and let the door close behind you. Turn around and look. See how it is shining, like a light bulb that has been lit inside of you radiating outward.

Δ From here, all this light energy is sent straight out to the person who is in need of it. Send the light energy to the outer area of the person's energy field. Through the twelve layers, layer by layer. See how the light energy moves like a wind and is distributed inward through all layers of the person's light body.

Δ Every time you encounter a stop, stay at that area, fill up with light energy, and remove the dark/black that resides in the field or in the physical body by drawing it out from the person's energy field. Move around and closer to the person if it feels like you need to.

Δ Eventually, the light energy reaches into the physical body. Then bring it in through the person's crown, through the entire body, and out through the feet. If you encounter a stop inside the body, draw it out, and ask to go back to the right layer in the light body to change the blockage, patterns, and memories. Ask for guidance.

Δ When you need to refill with more light energy, then just draw in more light from above, from below, and from your back, and gather the power in your heart.

Δ When the work is done, close the contact downwards and upwards. Also make sure to close it in your back. Give thanks for the work.

Eventually, when you have learned to use your heart in the right way, it is possible to use the technique to bring out the power through your hands. If your own heart is weak, then move the energy a little bit upwards, so the heart will not be too affected. Later on, when you have learned the technique well, it can be used remotely, and the preparation will only need to be a few breaths. You will be able to transform this technique so that you can give this sacred healing light to others simply by a handshake or at other moments when needed. Remember that you can heal everything in your path.

Exercise 4
Communicating with Nature

This exercise starts with parts from Exercises 2 and 3. Please practice these exercises a few times first. This exercise is used, for example, when you want to communicate with, feel, or exchange energies with animals, minerals, and other beings in nature.

△ Relax and breathe deeply. Feel how the air goes down through your trunk, down to your stomach. Feel how the breathing raises the vitality in your body.

△ Draw in the energies through your back, straight into your heart area. Imagine how you open up a door in your back where the energies flow in.

△ Feel that your heart is opened in depth and distributes the energy throughout your entire body.

△ Gather all the power around your heart. Start by asking the object for permission to do this exercise.

△ Now energetically step out of your body through your heart, and stand facing that which you want to connect your energy with. Look at the object, for example a tree, either with your eyes open or closed. Fantasize that you with your energy go towards and around the tree. Feel how you move your energy around the tree. At the same time, your energies will merge.

Go back to yourself, and see in front of you how you open the swinging doors straight into your heart. The door faces inward, to the depths of your body and the area around your heart. Step inside through the door, into yourself, and let the door close behind you. Turn around and start the communication and energy exchange. Feel how light and love leave you and enter into the tree, and how you get the unconditional love energy in return. Try to send out feelings, words, images, and thoughts, and start a communication.

Δ Don't forget to thank the tree after your meeting. Feel how you let out the energy of the tree by opening the doors in your heart again, step out of yourself, and then turn back alone.

Exercises 5 and 6
Redistributing Energy

These exercises are about gathering, controlling, and moving energy.

Exercise 5

If you learn how to redistribute energy, you will be able to move objects in the direction opposite to the force of gravity. This is done by the power of thought. Look upon the energy as air that can be moved. This exercise is a preparing exercise for moving the air, so that the force of gravity can be counteracted.

Δ Take a few deep breaths and relax your entire body. Sit comfortably, and please listen to relaxing music to reach a meditative state.

Δ Close your eyes and imagine that you are sitting in a room with a vacuum, a room entirely without matter. The room is totally free from air. Yet you can breathe in this vacuum, and you feel light and free.

Δ See that the door to this room is opened. Just slightly opened. A small amount of air starts to spread in the room. First, just as a breeze. You get surprised, because you can see the air. It sweeps in in front of you like a gray silk ribbon.

Δ The ribbon whirls slowly around your body, and you decide to try to gather the ribbon and get control of it by using your thought. By the power of thought, you grab one of the outer edges of the ribbon. The ribbon folds, but stays in front of you and stops whirling around your body.

Δ Now, gather the ribbon so that it folds into a flat piece of cloth in front you. When you start to get control of the piece of cloth, you let the door be opened a little bit more. More air now streams into the room, and you take control over it in the same way as above. This time, put the cloth under the previous cloth.

Δ You puff up the first piece of cloth so there is room for the new one underneath. Continue in the same way by bringing in more and more air, and let more and more pieces of cloth puff each other up.

Exercise 6

Now it is time to continue Exercise 5. You should practice that exercise many times before you proceed with Exercise 6.

Δ Keep a burning candle nearby. See the increasingly packed air in front of you. Now imagine how you start to play with these pieces of cloth by puffing them upwards and downwards. Let them also go around you, above, and below you.

Δ While playing with them, try all the time to add more air from the door, which is now half open and continuously lets in more air, little by little.

Δ Now focus for a short moment on the candle that you have lit. See how the air mass touches the candle without putting it out. Ask the air mass to adopt the vibration of the candle and see how the fire starts to vibrate at the same pace as the air mass. The air mass will simultaneously take the shape and color of the fire. See how everything vibrates at the same pace.

Δ After a while, let that which we call the piece of cloth puff the candle lightly, so that it moves forward a few millimeters on the table. Let the second piece of cloth push the first. See how the third pushes the second, which pushes the first, and so on.

Δ You will eventually be able to move the candle around on the table in any direction you want. Your thought easily changes the direction of the air mass. When you master this, you will also master the law of gravity.

Exercise 7
Energy Exercise that Prepares You for Future Energy Work

In order to learn to create, strengthen, and managing energy, you can start using the energy ball. This is an exercise that many of you recognize. Step one is to learn how to feel and find one's energy ball and transport it into the body and other things in order to heal and refill with energy. Step two is to learn how to release energy to irradiate and to create a power station that gives energy. Before you start playing with the ball, prepare yourself with Exercise 1 (open your heart and concentrate the energy) and take in the energy of Prime Creator from your back. Then open up your heart chakra by standing in front of yourself, and step back into your body to your heart area through the swinging doors that are opened straight into your heart.

Δ Place your hands in front of you. Gather the energy between them and feel how the energy becomes stronger and stronger through your thought and intention.

Δ Play with this ball that you have created, by making it so huge that it fills up the entire room or by making it tiny and intense. Throw the ball between your hands.

Δ Create a triangle between your hands and your heart. See how the ball arises within this triangular field by using your thought and intention.

Δ Put the ball inside a physical crystal. Focus on the crystal. Its frequencies can make the ball become more physical, as the crystal's light and sound can illuminate your energy ball. Practice trying to merge your energy ball with the crystal.

Δ Insert your energy ball into your physical body, with the intention that it shall heal and purify your body where needed.

Part 4

Thoth's Twelve Pyramids of Creation

Introduction

What I will now tell you happened after the fall of Atlantis, about 16,000 years ago. Twelve of us left Atlantis and spread to different locations on Earth to establish new civilizations. Our mission was to preserve the knowledge from Atlantis and Lemuria and to provide the opportunity for present-day humans to take back and remember again the knowledge from that time. Thus, it is the knowledge from Atlantis and Lemuria that form the basis for the Matrix that this part of the book is about.

This knowledge was hidden, in that Atlantis fell and the consciousness level of humanity was lowered so that they would be able to live and work in the third density level. Twelve pyramids of light were brought down into physical form on the planet. One could say that these pyramids came from another Universe and were manifested through what you call the void or the vacuum. They created a physical reality for souls to experience and to acquire knowledge and experiences from.

The pyramids were then raised to a higher frequency and are nowadays not distinguishable to the human eye. They still remain in this higher frequency on the third density plane, but will be visible to you. They form an energy grid that surrounds the entire globe in a beautiful check pattern, like the colors and the patterns in a kaleidoscope. The energy grid is a Matrix, an information pattern, containing both you and the story of creation for the entire Universe. The grid links together everything on and outside the Earth.

At the time of the fall of Atlantis, I went together with my spouse, priests, and priestesses to what you today call Egypt to take part in the creation of the sacred Pyramid of Cheops and the Matrix itself with the twelve etheric pyramids. The Pyramid of Cheops creates a portal from the Earth to the Matrix and further up through the galaxy to the Universe and Prime Creator. It is a mirror image/copy of the etheric pyramids that exist outside the physical plane. They are all interlinked through the energy portal that the Pyramid of Cheops constitutes. This

106

also functions as a large physical clock on your planet that, among other things, interacts with what you know as magnetism and gravity, and it also maintains the illusion of time, as it is a marker, a geophysical timepiece, on Earth. I have come through this pyramid many times, in many different forms, to guide and to teach.

The twelve pyramids each contain three unique frequencies that in total give thirty-six unique creational forces. These thirty-six creational forces all have different qualities and patterns. They used energies of light and frequency tones from crystals to create and manifest physical form, matter on Earth. Each pyramid, thus, has its unique program, and they all have different meanings and purpose. It is these programs that are now accessible and possible for everyone to reach.

The Atlantean and Lemurian eras are also forming the basis of many different peoples and cultures on Earth. We who left Atlantis all brought with us different specialized knowledge that came to characterize the cultures of the new civilizations. In all parts of the world there are a variety of differences between the cultures, but also many similarities in consideration of man, Earth, and the Universe. This depending on what was chosen to be preserved through the ages. Just look upon the differences between Oriental knowledge about the physical body compared to that of the West. This knowledge in Asia is very old, whether it is Vedic, Japanese, or Chinese. The knowledge of healing in energy form has always existed in some form in all cultures since the time of Atlantis.

All human beings have carried the Atlantean knowledge within themselves, but have not understood that they can open up to it. Instead, a few enlightened individuals have been allowed to perform ceremonies and healing.

There are many who have hidden, encoded, genetic memories from my teachings that are awakened in this time. These people will lead and pave the way so that all humans are given the opportunity to awaken their own codes and memories. This chapter is given to you as a tool for everyone to awaken the hidden knowledge again.

Through the thought and consciousness of the thirty-six creational forces, physical forms were created based on geometric patterns. These physical forms are interconnected and follow the cycles until the end of time. These cycles were to be known as the Cycles of Time. They were to be experienced in the everyday life of every evolved civilization, on both large and small scale.

The Cycles of Time were calibrated from the number twelve, based on the twelve Pyramids of Creation. The mechanism in these cycles was to be circular and seen as wheels within wheels, or clocks within clocks, to mark cycles within cycles. These cycles both have their beginning and their end within their own creation. A cycle is an eternal circulation. An example of cycles within cycles is a decade, which is a cycle, a gear, which holds within itself ten smaller gears, ten years. Every year, then, is a cycle of its own, that in turn holds within itself twelve smaller gears, the months. Every month is an even smaller gear that in turn holds even smaller cycles in the form of weeks, days, hours, minutes, and seconds. I hope that through this example you understand the term cycles within cycles and that all cycles have a beginning and an end. At every end, a new cycle is started, and there is rebirth within each cycle in eternity. Other examples of cycles are the great inhalation and exhalation of the Universe, the birth and death of the physical body of man, cell regeneration, and seasonal changes.

When the great Matrix of thirty-six creational forces was completed, an opportunity emerged for many more souls to start their life cycles on the planet.

Every single human being on Earth has keys to collect in this Matrix. There is a key to conquer in each pyramid for you to be able to develop to a high level and help yourself, the Earth, the people, and all other living things on the planet. The keys include thirty-six frequencies, three from each pyramid, based on the Holy Trinity. The keys will open hidden higher knowledge in you that you were born with and carry in your subconscious mind. Altogether, the pyramids hold the answers to all the questions, reflections, and thoughts that you have ever had as Earth humans.

By using the encoded keys, you will be able to open up your hearts and the doors that have hidden those messages, which exist in your subconscious and which your Higher Self is a carrier of. You will also receive the deepest understanding and awareness of your existence and be given the opportunity to reach total harmony. I open a master key in each pyramid, and you can open yours whenever you want, by entering the respective pyramid in a meditative state. All the frequencies of the pyramids reach all the way down to the center of Mother Earth, and all the way up to Prime Creator and further up into the Universe.

The pyramids contain Cycles of Time in eternity. Time does not exist. On Earth, linear time was created to make your existence comprehensible. It is an illusion. You will get an understanding of this when you receive the keys, especially key number one from Pyramid 1.

When you let go of controlling time, you will also be able to use all your lives, all that you have experienced, to free yourself in your present existence.

You can go into and out of the pyramids at any time, since time does not exist. Everything exists at the same time, here and now. Then there is neither any yesterday. This means that every day is a clean sheet. For you to be able to heal yourself, it is therefore of great importance to let go of what has been, and be in the now.

The twelve pyramids are the foundation of this grid, this Matrix, whose energy is sustained by a large number of physical buildings and knowledge from different civilizations all over the Earth. I speak of maybe more than one hundred and fifty thousand pyramids, buildings, temples, sacred mountains, and so on that affect the energies in addition to the twelve etheric pyramids.

The pyramids form triangles in a grid above the Earth. Imagine the Matrix like a lid above and around the Earth. There are branchings between the Earth and the subtle pyramids, like tunnels connected to the grid. All transportation of energy occurs via special openings, channels, or tunnels. These are located all over the Matrix, all the way down to Mother Earth.

You can learn how to move energies, handle solid energies, and change the polarity, and also to master the law of gravity, levitate, and move in time and space with the power of thought. This knowledge now opens up again. The only things that can prevent you from acquiring it are your fears and blockages.

If you draw the twelve pyramids, you will discover that spaces in between them appear. These intervening spaces have weaker frequencies, but strengthen the energies in the grids, thanks to the different buildings, stone circles, and sacred places on Earth.

Some of the eras of the etheric pyramids have ebbed away, but the knowledge and the frequencies remain. Some have made themselves more distinct, and others are about to thrive. Nowadays there are not really any highly advanced cultures in the Central and South American Maya and Machu Picchu empires. But their memories and knowledge remain. If you open your keys correctly you will understand exactly what I mean. Since linear time does not exist, these highly advanced cultures are thriving right now, aren't they? If the knowledge, approach, and experiences of all civilizations are compiled to one unit, we get The Book of Knowledge, the highest truth.

When you look for the pyramids, you have to do it on different levels. Open your senses and receive that which comes to you. As I mentioned earlier, this is a form of process of creation, an inner journey for each person. In order to reach these frequencies and keys it is important that you purify yourself on all planes—physically, psychologically, emotionally, and spiritually.

First, create your own lifeline before you begin to work with the frequencies of the pyramids. Your traumas, fears, and blockages from this and past lives may need to be cleansed and purified first. The more purified you are on all levels, the easier it will be for your physical body to receive the information and be raised in frequency before the coming transformation.

This Matrix is an aid for you and your development. It has not been possible to open up earlier, because it is only now that you are receptive to this information. If you continue to believe that you are trapped, then it is your own inner nets and imprints that hold you in that belief. It is very important to search in past lives to bring forth and release those existences where you had power. If you bring forth the power and the strength that is retrieved there, your weakness will lessen automatically. You can draw strength from positive incarnations, not just seek out and clear away blockages.

Every pyramid has a guardian. The first pyramid, which is my own and I am the guardian for, lies over Egypt, right above and peak-to-peak with the sacred Pyramid of Cheops.

If you enter this pyramid in a meditative state, imagine that you go into the lower part of the Pyramid of Cheops and travel in a spiral of light up to the second chamber. When you reach the chamber, you open a door and enter the sacred Crystal Room of tones, sound, and light. The first sound of the Universe exists in this room, the sound that was created in what you call the Big Bang. The entire room is covered with crystal that reflects its light in prisms. In there you can easily calibrate yourself, increase your vibration to a higher frequency, and then also at the same time automatically enter the second chamber of the first etheric pyramid, as they lie peak-to-peak, like an hourglass. Start from this room when you are going to enter the other eleven pyramids.

Each one of you can work with these pyramids on your own or in a group. You can wander in and out of them every day. You can, for instance, work with one pyramid per month. Feel free to do what you feel is the best for yourself.

Every time you enter a pyramid your body is affected by the frequencies, you are calibrated to the right vibration and open up all or part of the knowledge from the pyramid using the key that you receive. There is sacred knowledge that I and others have written down and that has to be brought to light.

You can never make any mistakes when you visit the pyramids. Remember that the power of thought is enormous and affects your whole situation every day. When you, for example, decide to enter Pyramid 3, you will be there automatically. Your experiences might differ completely from the experiences of others. You can experience totally different things, and nothing is wrong. Everything is right, as long as you have the intention to visit Pyramid 1, 2, or 3, and so on.

But you should always enter Pyramid 1 first and from there continue to the eleven others. Otherwise, it is like losing the foundation or the connection, so to speak, that I have created etherically to get to the different pyramids.

So enter the Pyramid of Cheops, which is the great entrance and exit to and from the Matrix. Walk into it, see it with your mind's eye, go up to the Crystal Room and choose which pyramid you want to enter, and you will get there just by having the thought. All your experiences will naturally be different. You do not need to know where the pyramid is located, or what it does. You can just enter it as it is or ask for permission to enter the pyramid that you have the need to visit right now.

#	Pyramid	Key
	Summary of Thoth's Twelve Etheric Pyramids of Creation	
1	Egypt, The Cycles of Time Begin	The Big Bang, the descending transformation, sacred geometry, time as linear, cosmic laws, light, and primordial sounds.
2	Middle East, The Tree of Life, The Programs Start	The cradle of civilization, healing on all levels, the history of man, light-darkness, the stairs in the Tree of Life.
3	Europe, Mythologies and Tales, The Book of Life	The library with all tales and myths, your tales/lives, all is illusion, change of negative tales, creating.
4	Atlantis, Illusion, A Tale from the Book of Life	Creating with light and sound, the battle, light-darkness, karma, forgiveness, intuition, work with spirit, purpose of life.
5	Lemuria, The Pacific Ocean, A Tale from the Book of Life, Ascension	Knowledge of different dimensions, raising in frequency, awareness of higher experience levels. Divine meetings.
6	Tibet, The Book of Knowledge, Sacred Texts	Sacred scripts, cosmic knowledge from all civilizations, hidden knowledge, spiritual masters and teachers.
7	Australia, Dreamtime, Subconciousness	The knowledge of accessing memories and hidden knowledge through sleep, problem solving, remembering the teachings of the dreamtime.
8	Antarctica, The South Pole, Extraterrestrial Contact	The portal to other planetary systems, guidance on arrival, extraterrestrial creating, cooperation and inspiration.
9	Arctic, The North Pole, Laws of Nature	Balancing of the poles and consciousness, meltdown shift, the power of thought, knowledge bank, understanding the laws of nature.
10	Peru, Machu Picchu, Emotions	All feelings together create the only true one: Love. letting go of adaptation, having trust, forgiveness.
11	Mesoamerica, Maya, Synchronization	The understanding of the entire Pyramid Matrix, reach higher consciousness, union of all wisdom and knowledge, your natural state.
12	New York City, Completion, Transitions	The journey home, the transition, ascension, the feminine principle, closing of the circle, the beginning and the end, the evolution.

Pyramid 1
The Cycles of Time Begin

The program starts with the first of the twelve pyramids, which contains the pattern for all that exists. It has a very strong frequency on all planes. Here exist keys to understanding of linear time.

The pyramid over Egypt is associated with the hourglass and with time and illusion. Here the fundamental tone of Prime Creator, the sound of the Big Bang, is found. From this primordial sound, all that exists is created through sacred geometry. These geometrical patterns are the origin of all form and manifestation, and they provide the conditions for the creation of the other pyramids.

From here the patterns for the laws of nature, such as time and space and cause and effect, were created. As a result of the Big Bang, soul atoms were thrown out and were divided into seed atoms. By that, duality came into existence. From the seed atoms, primary seeds are created, which in turn divide into five parts, or elements, that are needed for something to exist, according to the laws of your planet. This penta-partition is created every day in man. This is a cell division that is constantly ongoing in the human body. Thus, the seed was created from the seed atom at the Big Bang. One could say that it happened from the primary drop of Prime Creator. Everything is created in the same way: the Universe, the Milky Way, the Earth, and Man. From this, you can understand creation and the descending transformation. The thirty-six frequencies create your life pattern. Out of this, the little seed has the opportunity to be transformed down and become materialized into a human body with a solid form.

The Cycles of Time started here, and as the guardian of time, I was to perpetuate an illusion of these time cycles. It is my task to recalibrate each time cycle when time switches to a new space or a new time dimension. To mark these time cycles the Pyramid of Cheops was created as a geophysical clockwork on the surface of the Earth. The Matrix is connected to and kept together by means of the sacred Pyramid of

Cheops that constitutes the hub for all energy pathways in the Matrix.

In the second chamber of crystal, light, and sound you can meet me, your guides, or other energies that are currently important to you. Here you can go to refill yourself with energy if you are tired and need new power. Here is the starting point for you to access all other pyramids.

All the laws of the Universe are created through these frequencies, of light and darkness. Both of these polarities are equally important. It is man who has changed the basic idea of these and created an image that it is the dark forces that act in the dark. You achieve balance when darkness and light harmonize side by side.

But the most important thing here is the understanding of time. Linear time was created so that you would be able to live in a comprehensible context. When you fully reach the understanding of time as nonlinear, an enormous insight is opened that removes many limitations in you.

As mentioned earlier, the physical form of the first pyramid exists on Earth in the form of the Pyramid of Cheops, and its etheric form, which you will work with, is located peak-to-peak with it. The energy goes through the pyramid and into the Earth's innermost core.

To Visit Pyramid 1

Are you ready to come along on a little tour to receive your keys and calibrate your frequency with the sacred frequencies of this pyramid? It is, as previously stated, the most important pyramid in order for you to gradually be able to continue working with the frequencies that are available in the other eleven pyramids. I will take you to a place that is very warm, to Egypt, and lead you to the great physical Pyramid of Cheops. Right above this pyramid is the more subtle, and to the eye invisible, Pyramid 1 (which eventually, however, will be visible to the naked eye). To achieve total healing on the cellular level and in the smallest atom in your physical bodies, the first step is to reach the second chamber, the so-called Crystal Room. It exists simultaneously

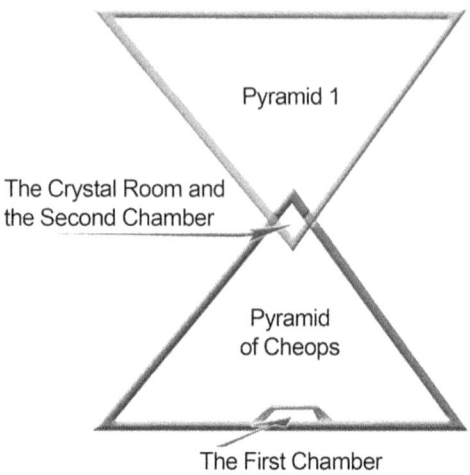

Pyramid 1

The Crystal Room and
the Second Chamber

Pyramid
of Cheops

The First Chamber

and at the same place both in the Pyramid of Cheops and in Pyramid 1. They exist at the same place, but they have different frequencies.

In a little while, you will open the door and go into the room of crystal. The second chamber, the room of sound and tones. Imagine how the walls of the room are covered by the purest crystal, and how crystal formations of all kinds and shapes are everywhere inside this room.

If you listen attentively, you will be able to hear the tones of the crystals, the fundamental tones of the Universe, but also all the other sounds and frequencies that exist in creation.

In order to open the key to the deepest knowledge for healing, it may be of importance to sing forth these tones.

Also, meet the light that is sent out from the crystals. There are light prisms everywhere in this hall, and you will be able to see many colors and combinations of colors from the entire color spectrum. Make the most of your time in chamber two.

When you are to enter the chamber, you shall focus on and keep your thoughts on the idea that everything will be changed and re-transformed to the fundamental vibration that you will carry in your continuing work on Earth. When you eventually come into the chamber, you shall imagine that there is a comfortable place for you to sit to take in the tones and sounds. Some will perceive them, while others will not hear anything. But your body will be transformed or, so to speak, be recalibrated to the fundamental frequency you are created to vibrate in. When your body has been recalibrated, you will automatically reach the etheric chamber in Pyramid 1. During their lives, many have created physical disease, psychological instability, or emotional suffering by deviating from their fundamental frequency and recalibrating their vibrations in the physical body.

Possibly you will get to meet an energy that is important to you in particular and who you can communicate with. Sometimes when you visit the room you will meet me, but you may also meet your guides or other persons, souls, or important energies that you need to be in contact with right now.

Meditation Exercise 1

Sit comfortably.

Imagine within yourself that you are in Egypt, with the Pyramid of Cheops straight ahead of you.

You get closer and closer and sense the frequencies of the pyramid.

Take in the atmosphere that surrounds the great sacred pyramid and feel its power.

Walk up to the pyramid and start to go around this large stone construction to look for your individual entrance, the one that is particularly for you to use.

If you do not find an opening, then imagine one.

When you have found your entrance, stand in front of it.

Now, take a step into the perfectly silent and dark pyramid.

However, you will not perceive it as dark, since you now have an inner vision.

You can clearly see what's in front of you.

Walk a few tentative steps into the pyramid. Right now, you are in Chamber 1 in the base of the Pyramid of Cheops.

Visualize or see that you now have a spiral of white light in front of you that circulates around and around.

The light from the spiral becomes stronger and you are drawn toward it.

Just step into the spiral and follow along in its turns.

Feel how you travel deeper inward and at the same time upward.

It goes around, and you travel with this spiral of light that will take you straight up toward the second chamber that lies just below the top of the pyramid.

Your entire light being becomes taller and taller as you travel faster inward and upward.

The speed slows down and you now catch a glimpse of the end of the spiral.

Just take a step out and visualize how you stand in front of a large doorway or a portal.

It may have any shape and also consist of various materials.

Please, open the door.

Step in and shut the door behind you.

Find a comfortable place in the room.

Focus on the thought that you shall raise in frequency and level.

You will now automatically be calibrated in frequency and reach the identical Crystal Room in Pyramid 1.

Now sit for a moment in the frequencies of sound and light, and open yourself to what comes.

Be aware that you are receiving what you need at this very moment, even though you may not have a clear perception of anything.

Have trust and love in what comes.

It is time to leave this room, but be aware that you can return here at any moment.

Now you must return to a lower frequency.

Feel how the body is calibrated down again to normal frequency.

Say goodbye to the room, open your door, and step out so that you stand in front of the spiral that leads you back to the base of the physical Pyramid of Cheops.

Now step into this spiral and travel in the opposite direction back down.

Feel how you tumble around and how your body becomes taller and taller.

Feel how you slow down and land inside the base of the great sacred pyramid.

Take a few steps and then go out through the entrance.

Could you hear the tones and perceive the light in the Crystal Room? All sound and light contain a frequency. You might perceive the tones as divorced from reality and very high pitched. Everyone can hear, but it takes practice to do so. Eventually, as you rise higher in frequency, the sounds will be clearer. Then you will perceive them more easily. Earthly humans will change their hearing and will perceive sounds that are not audible in the current situation. However, you have been affected by the sounds in the Crystal Room, even though you couldn't perceive the tones and light of the crystals. You get access to the key and the energies, even though you find it difficult to visualize the exercise. Remember that you can practice and go back whenever you want. You have now received at least one frequency from the first pyramid in the program.

You can go into this room for five minutes, five, six, seven times per day, and by this at the same time remind yourself to think right, to open your heart, and to start using your own inner knowledge. Just sit in this sacred room until you feel complete. The other pyramids in the program include all the knowledge that you carry within yourself, but for which you need the keys to open up and get access to the knowledge. If you need me, call upon me and I will come to you; simply receive the energy and meet me.

Pyramid 2
The Tree of Life ... The Programs Start

The second pyramid is located in etheric form above what you call the Middle East, in a large pattern. Every pyramid has a guardian, and Amun is the guardian of this pyramid. A very powerful energy.

It is from the frequencies of this pyramid that the story about the first humans arose. Their existence created a pattern, a basic pattern for man and the civilizations to follow. This pyramid includes the Earth's creation story, all the way from the Big Bang to your stories of creation, including the one you know about Adam and Eve and their bloodline. Here are the programs and the patterns, gathered in the Tree of Life, of all earthly stories, myths, and illusions that have ever existed. The sacred symbols and patterns of this creation were genetically encoded into those who would come to be part of this land. It is these souls who are awakening at the end of this time cycle to lead others into the next creation. A new Tree of Life will be born out of this pyramid.

It was here that the Ego was formed, took power over the mind, and created conflict. This has led to suffering in this region, and it is here that the forces of light and darkness will play out their battle and dissolve imprints from these early struggles for power. Much blood has been shed in this region by those who have lived in this frequency range. The mission of the humans here has been to keep and perpetuate the story of creation. They have carried this pattern like the feeling of a burden throughout this time cycle. The frequency of the pyramid now affects this bloodshed, which will disappear in the New Age. The battles will continue until the end of this cycle and until the beginning of the new Golden Age of Light.

When you travel through the geometric shapes of the pyramid matrix, you will understand how the first man and woman were created. The admittance to Pyramid 2 will open up keys for your personal story of creation, and this means that whenever you want, from now on, you can return, work, and get answers to your own life situation. Thereby you can also process all the traumas, all the experiences you carry with you since the beginning of time. That is mighty, my friends! This is so huge that you cannot yet grasp what it is you are doing. Man has not had access to this ability since the advanced civilizations of Lemuria and Atlantis operated upon Earth.

The frequency of this pyramid also holds the very deepest form of healing frequencies. When you reach this frequency, you can find the keys for all healing. Amun will embrace you and take you into the pyramid, where you will find healing from everything you have endured on all your Earth journeys. There will be a new beginning. Darkness returns to light, and souls will be free and healed.

For several years here on Earth, I have talked to humans about purifying and healing on all levels and planes. Clear out all traumas, both from this life and previous incarnations from the perspective you are in today, and with the ability of knowledge that you carry right now. This is in order for the transition into the higher vision and the higher knowledge to operate more smoothly.

You can use the Tree of Life, which exists inside the pyramid, to release imprints, fears, and traumas. When you reach the pyramid, you will find a large staircase that leads you up the trunk inside the Tree of Life. Follow the stairs and play in them. You can use them in many different ways. It is only your imagination that limits you.

It is important to be human, to be in focus here and now, and not to escape life. Use the time you have to mold yourself and follow the route choice you once made.

If you do not have your line and your path is not clear for you, then it is time today to make up your mind. Set your focus, enter this pyramid, and ask for guidance. Imagine that this tree will show you the way you yourself chose to walk, to the task you have in this life right here and now. You yourself can create whatever you want in this pyramid and see what you need to see at the time when you are there. To take in all the information at once may be too much.

Since your birth, you have lived in a frequency that is relatively heavy, but Earth is now on its way up to a higher frequency, which means easier flow on all levels.

To Visit Pyramid 2

Always begin by going in through the earthly Pyramid of Cheops and on up into the etheric Pyramid 1. Calibrate your body so that it, so to speak, is raised automatically. When you calibrate into the tones and the light, you will automatically reach the sacred chamber in the etheric first pyramid, the one I call the Crystal Room. After that, I will lead you to the second pyramid.

You can ask this pyramid, Amun, and the Tree of Life to open up and show you all the memories and feelings you carry that mess things up for you and make you be and act like the human you really are not. Feelings that you have hidden in your unconscious shall come to light so that you are able to let them go. Then go to Pyramid 1 to shower in the light and sound and to replenish with light and love for yourselves.

As you will now get access to the key in this pyramid (which includes not only the knowledge of creation but also the Tree of Life and healing on all levels), so it is good that you feel stable and in form before entering. In that you will get access to very high energies, it is important that you feel strong. If you then continue working in these particular frequencies on your own, it is important that you feel mentally strong and are not affected by any stimulants or similar drugs.

When you walk up the stairs in the Tree of Life, you can imagine that the branches growing out symbolize all your incarnations. By opening the key, you can also at the same time get all knowledge about creation.

The healing will occur on a plane that is high, inside and out. Inside the pyramid, you will be able to open your hearts and get the opportunity to purify yourselves on all planes from all times in an instant.

It is time for humanity to return to this pyramid to be cured and healed in the womb of creation.

You will have one of my co-workers with you during the entire process. Just breathe, and witness inner images in front of you. No matter how much or little you experience inside the pyramid, you will receive the key.

Meditation Exercise 2

Sit comfortably.

Breathe deeply and with slow breaths.

See how you walk forward until you stand before the great Pyramid of Cheops in Egypt.

Just walk around it until you find an opening. Enter the base.

It is dark, so open up your inner vision.

I now send down the spiral of light that will help you travel up to the second chamber in this pyramid.

Just walk into this spiral of light and feel how you now travel around, around, and upward.

Feel how your light body becomes taller.

Feel how the speed is slowed down, and feel that you put your feet down on solid ground.

You now stand in front of a door. This door leads you into the crystal chamber.

This is the hall of tones, where all the fundamental tones are and where the story of creation begins.

Just open the door and enter, and you might meet me.

Possibly you will perceive me or perhaps even see me.

Choose a suitable place to sit.

My co-workers will now help you, together with the crystals in this room, to be calibrated to a higher frequency.

You fill yourself up and receive these three sacred frequencies.

You are about to be calibrated up to the sacred frequencies in Pyramid 1.

Just see in front of you the shimmering color spectrum that these crystals create.

If you can perceive a tone, it is good.

The crystals might adopt a somewhat indistinct shape.

Just feel how this power is coming toward you.

We will now fold over the top of the Pyramid of Cheops.

You can now in your mind's eye see the sky, up in the ceiling where the top should have been found.

Through this opening, I now bring down the sacred spiral of light.

You enter this spiral and will travel together with me to Pyramid 2.

Feel how you travel, how your body is drawn out to a tall lightbody and that it goes fast.

You slow down, and you now find yourself at the base of Pyramid 2.

There is a door that we enter together.

This pyramid is a very sacred place.

It includes all darkness and all light on Earth.

The story of creation that you yourself have created and that Earth has gone through in the Universe.

You are now in the base, in the middle, and you stand by a staircase. This staircase will lead you upward.

The staircase is right in the middle of the Tree of Life.

You stand at the base of the trunk of the Tree of Life.

You take no steps yet.

Every time you enter this pyramid you have a choice: to enter your Tree of Life or the tree of the story of creation.

Your Tree of Life has branches. You can choose to walk out on any of them or to continue up the trunk.

The branches include all your existences.

If you choose to go out on the branches, you will briefly both see and get access to your respective existence.

Focus on your heart; feel its vibration and how the heart opens.

Feel how the key is turned around and how you keep this key forever in your heart.

The key opens your heart before every meeting with your creation.

When you walk up the stairs, you will be able to experience the entire creation, from the Big Bang up until now. Now walk on.

Just continue walking, and take a few minutes to walk in this tree.

You will now slowly turn around and go down, go back and down the stairs.

Walk step by step down to the bottom.

Say goodbye to the guardian of the pyramid.

Travel the spiral in the opposite direction back to Pyramid 1, until you reach the Crystal Room.

Refill yourself with light and sound, and feel how you are slowly calibrated back slightly in frequency.

Open the door and take the next spiral or elevator down, to the base of the Pyramid of Cheops.

Step out of the pyramid and come back.

If you carry fears, you can work with these in the Tree of Life. Among other things, it is your fears you are processing when you work with your timeline. Here you have the opportunity to work with your Line, to purify and cleanse your traumas from all your lives.

You can enter the Tree of Life and decide in advance that the steps make up your lifeline. For each step you take in the staircase, you are purified and healed from every trauma at each age. Start at your present age, and take another step to reach the previous year. Then take a step for every year back to year zero.

This is another way of working with your lifeline, where you do not need to use paper and pencil. If you carry fears that you need to work with, my friend, pray in advance that they shall let go of you.

All the emotions that you meet, all the traumas that have come upon you, and all blockages from previous years, you just let them be swept away. You can even collect all the blockages in a bucket, take it back to the Crystal Room, and leave it to Mother Earth, who takes care of it. Never forget to refill with light and sound before you leave the Crystal Room.

When you eventually have reached the crown of this tree, you will also be healed. You have then passed all your existences. This does not prevent you from entering the Tree of Life over and over again, as it starts a new time and new events that can give you feelings and thoughts that need to be cleansed and purified.

This pyramid includes the darkness and the light. If we can heal this era, then all humans will live in unity, peace, and harmony with each other. For each step you take, not only are you yourself cleansed, but the whole world is also gradually freed from the destructive encompassing power.

Being human has for a long time been experienced as difficult. You will observe that everything becomes lighter and simpler, as your thoughts will turn into action and bounce right back to you.

Pyramid 3
The Book of Life ... Mythologies and Tales

Pyramid 3 was placed over Europe in order to create mythologies and tales for souls to experience. It holds frequencies for your imagination and your personal myths. Here you download all forms of creating. The pyramid contains a great library, with many beautiful halls filled with papyrus scrolls, books, wisdom, and tales. These patterns are repeated in cycles, each with its own characters as elements of a collected work with no beginning or end. The fabric constantly creates new stories.

The guardian of the pyramid goes under the name of Triogenes, the Storyteller. He is the one who can capture the imagination of one soul, or all souls, as he weaves the patterns of his tales and mythologies from the energies of the Matrix. At the moment, these three strong frequencies affect all the choices of myths that you have ever spun since the Big Bang.

In the fabric of each mythology are the keys to the process of creation. These mythologies have been regarded as the Great Mysteries of the creation of humanity, and they came to take form as plays in different dimensions, where souls can choose one or more roles.

This pyramid includes all your personal tales, lives, and myths that you have ever participated in since the beginning of creation. Humans are born into this frequency to use beautiful and developing lives over and over again on Earth. It is about developing your souls in many varying physical forms to acquire many different experiences.

You always choose your own lives, tales, and myths, based on what you need to develop.

All is an illusion, but the illusion is also all, so then, what is reality and what is imagination?

To Visit Pyramid 3

When you go into the library you can choose an existence from here that is favorable for you to experience. You can also enter the pyramid for the purpose of trying to shape a new future.

Here you can also find patterns in the choices you have made so far. If you find less pleasant patterns, you can always rewrite your history and create new beautiful patterns instead.

So here you can create and weave new patterns and break old ones. You can create exactly what you wish by using your imagination and creativity for whatever you want. Here you can reformulate and change. Use your creativity and ability to create. There are no limitations.

The mythologies are not bound by space or time and can be experienced whenever you like.

When you step into this pyramid, you will be able to interact in all myths and tales simultaneously, by merely placing your consciousness in their fabric of patterns.

Many of my stories are written down and preserved in this library. Perhaps you and I can create a mythology or tale of our own. For in truth, All is Myth, Myth is All.

Meditation Exercise 3

Just relax and take a few deep breaths.

Close your eyes, relax, and feel that you are outside the sacred Pyramid of Cheops.

See how you walk around it, until you find your own entrance.

Step into the base and follow the spiral of light up to the second chamber.

Just feel how you step into the spiral of sacred light and sacred tones and follow along.

You are going around and up with it.

Feel how you become taller and taller in your light body until you slow down, step off, and stand in front of the door to the sacred Crystal Room.

Enter the door and find a place to sit down.

Just feel how you calibrate yourself up, higher and higher in frequency.

Feel how the tones and the light enter every cell.

You have now been calibrated up to the first pyramid, the etheric chamber of light and sound.

Now see how the ceiling opens, or a door with the number 3 opens, and the sacred spiral comes forth in front of you.

See how the spiral of light and sound continues from the pyramid and leads you on toward Pyramid 3.

Transport your Higher Self through the spiral.

Feel how your light body travels faster and faster, until you reach the base of Pyramid 3.

It contains a great library, with a great number of beautiful halls filled with books and wisdom. Halls filled with papyrus scrolls and myths.

Walk around in the halls until you find something that you might want to read, or find a place to sit to open your inner keys.

The information may come to you in different ways, not only through words to your physical body.

Stay here for a moment now.

When you feel ready, it is time to go back to the spiral, which takes you back to Pyramid 1.

Follow the spiral back, and sit for a moment in the sacred Crystal Room.

Refill yourself with light, sound, and love for yourself.

Then return down by opening the door and taking the spiral down, to the base of Cheops' physical pyramid.

Leave it when you are ready, and come back to the room.

You can experience many different events inside the pyramid and also feel strong physical sensations like nausea and euphoria.

I give an example from one of my students of how you can use the frequencies of the pyramid: She looked up a book from the library and asked for the answer to why she suffers from headache. There she got to experience an old life where she had died from an arrow through the eye. She then used her creative ability and saw herself die in another way in that life. Thus, she reconstructed her end of that life. This is an excellent way of changing and removing old imprints. What you affect and change in any of your past lives will affect all other lives, including your present one.

It is important always to refill with a light shower in the Crystal Room after visiting any of the pyramids.

No matter if you see, feel, or hear anything, you must trust that you will take part of the keys for imagination and creativity.

Pyramid 4
Atlantis, A Tale from the Book of Life ...
The Knowledge Becomes Hidden

Pyramid number four is located above the place you call Atlantis. It is the world of my origin. I am descended from this frequency and have been in Atlantis for a long time. I was the ruler of Atlantis for many years. This pyramid does not exist above any specific location.

The soul that oversees it goes by the frequency of Arlis Cochizel.

The Atlantean pyramid creates an illusion of realities along a time-line on Earth. Here the ability to see time as an illusion of past, present, and future was created. Through the crystal matrix of this pyramid, an evolvable race of humans was born. Here man started to evolve linearly with life after life, experience after experience. With this creation of a timeline, the illusion of what you call karma was also created.

In the Atlantean pyramid exists the pattern of how the destructive battle between the light and the dark was started. Light and darkness are each other's opposites, the feminine and masculine power. None of them can exist without the other. But man has created what you call evil, and associates this with darkness.

By using frequencies from this pyramid, the visible pyramids that exist at certain places on Earth were partially created. With the power of thought, energy was created and transformed on all different planes in such a way that one created exactly what was needed for the occasion and moment. Tones and sounds were used to create buildings, among other things. People teleported and transported themselves, both in physical and etheric form, wherever they wanted. Just like you are able to on the astral plane, they could split their consciousness on different planes and levels simultaneously. This knowledge existed in the evolved race of humans during the Atlantean era. My friends, this is stored in each one of you. Thanks to the sacred Matrix, you have the opportunity to bring forth this ancient knowledge.

If you can create with energy, then what prevents you now from developing your ability to create anything you want with energy? This knowledge still exists, and you now get full access to it. You will benefit from this when you work with healing. Some of you already work with these pyramid frequencies, with the tones, light, and sound of the crystals.

A large group of Atlanteans who were very skilled at this frequency work were from other places and civilizations. A smaller group of them worked diligently with developing and creating in the halls of the sacred crystal temple. The halls of this sacred temple subsequently became a factory for energy.

There are many reasons for the fall of Atlantis. It destroyed itself. Its inhabitants went too far in their creating. It began far back in time, about 16,000 years ago. Something I could call debris fell down on parts of Atlantis, debris in the form of meteors and the like, which damaged large parts of the area. This debris resulted in a sharp reduction of the Earth's energy field and its magnetism, something that also led to the weakening of the Earth's polarity. This was one of the events, and that's how it started.

In parallel, there were groups of individuals that initially created and developed with good intentions. However, the ego in a few of them grew strong, due to the power they possessed, and they became blind to the good intentions that their work was meant for from the beginning. For every moment that someone takes power from someone else, the ego grows. They developed their knowledge to a level that someone today could almost compare with what you call nuclear bombs. People became ill, and now I speak about ordinary people just like you. They started to feel bad and lost their knowledge and the ability to create.

One of my tasks on Earth today is to make man stop judging others, for each time you judge an individual in a human encounter, these old memories from this era are triggered, and your ego grows temporarily. Remember that everything you think and everything you do eventually rebounds back on you.

There was no other way out but to let Atlantis fall. If we had not placed the etheric pyramid grid over the Earth, then the Earth would not have made it. You would definitely not have managed the living that you have had the last few centuries here on Earth. The Earth now has to go up in frequency. Otherwise the memories from Atlantis will conquer your consciousness to the degree where the Earth can no longer exist. I say we, because I was, of course, not alone in doing this, but it is I who have been given the task to here and now inform you all about the Matrix and the pyramids.

Many people left the place and brought with them what they thought was the most important—the basic knowledge from Atlantis and Lemuria—to different places in order to create civilizations that still today use the knowledge in different ways. These wisdoms have been developed differently over the millennia into what they are today, just like your belief systems have developed in different places. When Atlantis sank, I brought with me my consort Seshat and our highest priests and priestesses in large spaceships, to create a new home and a new civilization. The new place was the land of Khem, known to you as Egypt. Here the great sacred Pyramid of Cheops was built as an image of the etheric pyramids.

I and others from Atlantis recorded and stored information in great libraries, in a place called Amenti. Amenti means "humanity."

Many have searched for this stored information in their quest to remember why they have come here and who they are. They feel that they have a greater purpose in this life and want to try to find out what that purpose might be.

To Visit Pyramid 4

Thanks to the Matrix, you can now open your keys to all knowledge that you acquired already at the time of Atlantis and Lemuria. You all existed during this time. You all have memories from these eras. Now it is important for each one of you to open up these memories and these keys. Enter the Atlantean pyramid with the imagination of and the illusion that your keys will be opened, and so you will let them be opened. The memories will come creeping, both day and night. You will be reminded of what has been and of the knowledge you carry with you in genetic form. In this pyramid frequency, you will gain insight on how to create from the light and sound of crystals, and also get knowledge of managing energy on all levels and creating by using energy and the power of thought. The Atlantean pyramid holds a great mythology from a time when the gift of working with intuition and the energy of spirit was used.

The frequencies from the pyramid give you a realization that there is no beginning, nor is there an end. Think of Atlantis and walk into the pyramid; you will know within yourselves where this pyramid is located. See Atlantis as an enormous place. You all have had a life in this place and will here get the opportunity for forgiveness on all levels. You will also gain insight into why this place went down.

I, Thoth the Atlantean, shall now take you to the Pyramid of Atlantis, so that you may experience all that you are. You will understand what happened in the game of light versus darkness, and you will remember what you must do.

You will also open up the key so that you can learn how to travel in time and space. Go inside the pyramid and into the halls, and feel how you slowly open up the key to this knowledge.

Enter these halls, meet the frequencies, and get, if needed, the understanding of why you are here, why you walk the path you do. Ask to get all the answers you wish about what you want to know. Ask also to get the answers about light and darkness and why karma came into existence, why the civilization perished, and why you have incarnated on Earth here and now. You will also get an understanding of the illusion of linear time.

Open up the key so you can start using the powers that the crystal can bring.

Meditation Exercise 4

Just breathe.

Feel how you focus on your breathing around your heart.

Visualize in front of you how you see the sacred Pyramid of Cheops in its physical form.

Just walk towards it.

Walk around it until you find an opening that is intended for you.

When you find your opening, enter the base of the pyramid.

Go inside and see the sacred spiral shape of light and sound in the middle in front of you.

This spiral of light and sound will lead you inward and higher up in the pyramid.

Just step into the spiral and follow around.

Feel how it goes faster and faster, until you slow down and stop in front of a door.

This door leads you into the sacred chamber of crystal, light, and sound.

Just open the door, enter, and find a place to sit. Fill yourself up with energy from the tones and the lights of the Big Bang of origin, where creation began and started its descending transformation.

Fill up with light and see how the light is refracted in the prisms, how beautiful colors circulate around in the entire room.

Just sit and enjoy until the frequencies of the body have been raised.

For each moment you sit here, you will automatically calibrate yourself more easily, until you find yourself in the etheric Pyramid 1, in the room that is identical with the one you already sit in.

Everything might at the same time become more blurred, more vague.

Pyramid 1 lies peak-to-peak with the physical Pyramid of Cheops.

Here you can, whenever you want, call upon me, and also your guides.

Remember that you must return here between every entrance to any of the other pyramids.

You can return here in a meditative state whenever you want, for short moments, when you need a break in your daily life.

Now see how a door with the number 4 is created, or how the ceiling glides away, and how the spiral of light and sound appears and becomes visible.

Feel how you step into the spiral.

Join this spiral to Pyramid 4, to Atlantis.

You are transported around and around.

Now you slow down and land inside the base of the Atlantean pyramid.

This is a temple with halls and rooms of the purest crystal. These halls of crystal are in a bigger format than the Crystal Room you just left.

Both the walls and the ground you walk on are made of the most sacred crystal from the time of Atlantis. The prisms refract light in all colors.

You can look at yourself in the walls and let them talk to you.

Here you can now walk around for a while and see what you meet.

What memories are brought to life?

If you need to go through a forgiveness process, then ask for this.

Now walk around on your own, until you feel it is time to finish.

Go back to where you entered, and find the spiral of light.

Feel that you step into the spiral and slowly travel back in the opposite direction, to the second chamber in Pyramid 1, around and around.

Feel how you slow down and again find yourself in the second chamber in the Pyramid of Cheops.

Refill with light and sound in your body.

It is always important, especially if you have let go of something, to refill the void that has been created inside your physical body.

Just feel how you refill yourself and at the same time are calibrated down in frequency.

Leave what you have let go of in the Crystal Room.

Mother Earth will take care of it.

Then open the door, and take the spiral in reverse, back down to the base of the Pyramid of Cheops.

Just step out of the spiral, walk to the exit, and leave the Pyramid of Cheops behind you. Open your eyes and come back.

You have been in an image of the Sacred Temple of Atlantis, a temple that was so sacred that only a few inhabitants had access to enter this temple. Now the temple is open for all inhabitants and Earth people.

You can do this again on your own at any time. The sacred crystal temple is open for you.

Pyramid 5
Lemuria, A Tale From the Book of Life ...
Celestial Connections

The era and civilization that was called Lemuria existed before and parallel with Atlantis. These two tales from the Book of Life are chosen because they participated in the creation of it. Without these two, the Matrix would not exist. They both lived side by side, and the Lemurians were very aware of what took place in Atlantis and saw its fall coming. Several hundred years before Atlantis fell and the Earth went down into the third density level, the Lemurians ascended into the fifth density level. There they still exist on a high level.

Every density level has many planes and levels. It is the same journey that you and planet Earth will now have to make. This advanced civilization was at its greatest about 20,000 years ago, and even further back. They lived on a continent in the Pacific Ocean, and the inhabitants were a mix from different civilizations. The levels of consciousness differed, and people were on the fourth density level. At that time, there existed no form of "evil" whatsoever of the kind that Earth and its humans have endured on the third level.

Those who first inhabited Lemuria were the Sirians. Everyone knew each other, and they had major exchange amongst themselves. The Lemurians were just as advanced as the Atlanteans. They created with crystals, sound, and light, and lived in total balance and harmony. Their bodies were not as heavy and physical as those you have now. They could at any time adopt either a more dense or a more subtle form. They could change themselves and their consciousness, and they could, so to speak, pass the different dimensions (or as I call them, the levels) in an instant by their power of thought.

It was through their ability to control the brain and the inner flows of energy, that the Lemurians could so easily raise their frequency and bring with them what they needed. They could make their physical bodies gigantic, as these did not consist of such dense matter as yours do today. Also, the race of humans that lived in Lemuria had a lower density in their physical bodies, because they lived on a higher level. If only humanity could understand and believe that our Lemurian ancestors rose to those heights and that there is more than just the physical expression, then humans would be in readiness to move to the next level of consciousness.

The soul that oversees this pyramid goes by the frequency of Teco Porima. The pyramid grid is right now located over the Pacific Ocean, and has sometimes been viewed by passing sailors when they have moved between the different consciousness levels of reality on their voyages in the open seas.

The true nature of this pyramid is to maintain and enforce the awareness of higher levels of experience. The Lemurian pyramid creates illusions of different levels of reality. The pyramid is very subtle and has such high vibrations that it is almost transparent, jellylike in its shape. Its delicate, gentle frequencies affect man strongly. When you later visit this pyramid, you will probably feel that it is more subtle in its form. The Lemurians have always helped the Earth humans, and many of your guides come from there. The Lemurians have a very close cooperation with the people on Earth and are very eager to assist in the raisings that occur.

This frequency and this pyramid are very important for your development. In this pyramid frequency, you will gain insight about the Lemurian ascension and how you will be able to rise up to a new level. The frequencies from Lemuria are important, as you get all the inner information from there about working with different dimensions, planes, and levels. Also, how you can work from your physical body to different levels, to acquire knowledge and then come back to the level you are on. Pyramid 1 and 5 help you to remember this knowledge.

When you work with different frequencies, levels, and planes, then it is frequencies from this pyramid that you download. Some use this pyramid when they work with trance states; the body (Paula) does

140

this when she works with me. The pyramid is also about your inner dimensions, to center and balance your interior. When you reach inner balance, you also reach the outer. It is so simple: a micro and a macro cosmos.

When you ascend, you will bring many individuals that are connected with you, your family, your friends, your work colleagues, your neighbors, and so on. This includes all the people that are in your particular vicinity, and it will not happen from one day to another. Ascension occurs during a longer period. But you will first reach the frequencies of the fourth level before the higher ascension starts.

When you are able to love your fellow human beings you will automatically love yourself, because your feelings and thoughts are a direct reflection back to yourself. It is just like in the mirror image of the Lemurian pyramid, where you will not only see, feel, and experience reflections of all planes and levels, but also your interior.

To Visit Pyramid 5

You will change in form, lose your physical shell, and reach your light body. When you get rid of the shell, you will realize that you are very large in your light form. The experience may be that you feel very large in size, but sometimes also small.

You will pass different rooms in this pyramid and will see mirrors that reflect parts of realities that you are now ready to take in and that show the development from Lemuria to today's date.

Look into the mirrors that cover the walls and that show you who you are without physical form. You may experience your journey from the tiny seed to the divine cosmic being you are today, and that gives you strength and power. You may also meet light beings that help you to a higher frequency, both temporarily, but also later, when it is time for ascension.

Walk into and out of the halls of this subtle pyramid and look in the mirrors, see what the mirrors show you. It is flashbacks from the history of all earlier pyramids, but also flashbacks to all levels, Universes, and systems you have been on in your existences.

This pyramid may awaken feelings that are hard to deal with for some people, feelings that are not processed regarding the different planes and levels. Unprocessed feelings and situations that you have experienced in and between your past lives on different levels get in tune with you when you enter the pyramid. This may allow for feelings to be created that feel unpleasant or sad.

Be clear that this pyramid is perfectly pure; only love and light exist here.

You remember that I mentioned that in the previous pyramid, the fourth (Atlantis) were created light and darkness and what you call karma, which is not one of the laws of the Universe, but the invention of man. This does not exist in the frequencies around Lemuria. Here is only a pure mind to work with. Lemuria had already left the frequency of the Earth when the Matrix was created, and therefore has no influence in its pattern of what you call evil and destructiveness. Here you merely have the knowledge and understanding of the transformation, your Higher Selves, higher guides, and the communication with light beings from different levels. What you meet are reflections of your own inner memories and traumas, and these influence you.

The guardian of the pyramid sends words for you to always try to be here and now. Just live as a human being so that you can master the element earth and at the same time master your ego. Every moment that you are here and now, the memories from old wrongs will fade away. He will continue to work with you after you have received the key.

He says that all you need to do is to open your eyes, and you will see the different realities in front of you. But the condition is that you open your forehead chakra—your third eye—and your crown chakra. Then you will also take command over all other chakras that will be united and centered in your heart. In conjunction with the opening of the throat, the pituitary gland and the hormonal systems will automatically change and be balanced, and you will get access to the third eye in a new way. When you visit these frequencies, you will notice that your entire physical interior, including the chakra system and the organs, will be affected.

The most important thing is that you bring a wish to awaken the ability to rise in frequency. Ask to receive the keys and to get the help you need before you enter the pyramid. It is time to enter the Pyramid of Lemuria and cooperate with those that create this pyramid matrix.

Meditation Exercise 5

Just breathe.

Feel how you put focus on your breathing around your heart.

Feel that you release all thoughts that disturb you.

Just breathe in light and love from Prime Creator.

Visualize in front of you how you see the sacred Pyramid of Cheops.

Just walk towards it. Walk around it until you find an opening that is meant for you.

When you find the opening, enter the base of the pyramid.

Go inside and see the sacred spiral form of light and sound right in front of you.

This spiral of light and sound will lead you up, higher and inward, to the sacred second chamber.

Just step into the spiral and follow along, around and around.

Feel how you step into the spiral and travel upwards and upwards.

Feel how the light body becomes taller from the speed until it slows down, you take a few steps out, and stop in front of a door.

This door leads you into the sacred chamber of crystal, light, and sound.

Just open the door, enter, and find a comfortable place to sit.

Refill with energy from the tones and the light from the Big Bang of origin, where creation began and started its descending transformation.

Just fill yourself with light and see how the light is refracted in the prisms.

See how the beautiful colors circulate in the entire room.

Feel how the light and the sound from the crystal go into your physical body, into every cell, atom, and particle.

Just feel how you start to vibrate and rise in frequency.

For each moment you sit in the room, you will automatically be calibrated and raise in frequency, higher and higher, until you find yourself in the etheric pyramid number 1.

It's a room identical with the one you are now sitting in.

Everything might at the same time become more blurred and weaker.

Just sit and enjoy, until the frequencies of the body have been raised.

Remember that you have to return here in between every entrance.

You can return here when you need a break in your daily life, whenever you want to during the day, in a meditative state.

Now see how a door is created with the number 5 on it, or how the ceiling glides away, and how the spiral of light and sound becomes visible.

This spiral will now take you further up in frequency, higher and higher, to the Lemurian Pyramid 5.

You travel up and up and up, higher and higher, until you enter the base of this subtle pyramid.

Step off the spiral and go into the halls of crystal, which have a high vibration.

Just continue forward and see if you can find the mirrored walls or be guided to the information or the knowledge that it is time for you to receive in entering into this pyramid.

Ask to get to bring back the keys.

When you feel complete in the pyramid, go back to the base of this pyramid.

Find your way to the base of this pyramid until you find the spiral that takes you in the opposite direction, back down to the second chamber in Pyramid 1.

Please, step into the spiral that leads you back. Feel how you travel in the opposite direction until you again sit in a comfortable position in Pyramid 1.

Take a few seconds and fill yourself with light and sound from the crystal.

Feel how you heal yourself, absorb the light and the sound, and at the same time calibrate yourself down in frequency and come back.

Then go to the door, open it, and take the spiral in the opposite direction, down to the base of the Pyramid of Cheops.

When you reach the base, you can leave the Pyramid of Cheops and come back to a conscious state.

You have now received the keys for the knowledge to be transformed to a higher level and frequency in the Universe. Already now, you have the possibility to, whenever you want, pass whatever level or whatever plane you want to, and then return to the frequency of the Earth. When you are to pass between the different levels, first go to the Lemurian pyramid and ask to follow the pyramid. Let the pyramid open you up, and follow the divine cord or the golden ray that leads from Prime Creator through all levels, all the way down to Mother Earth. Choose to follow this cord to feel safe and secure. Follow the cord into the interior of Mother Earth or up to the higher frequency levels. Open your mind to meet other civilizations and light beings on your way, when you play with going into and out of this frequency.

You have, via the frequencies of the pyramid and this key, received the ability to transport yourself onward to higher levels outside this Universe.

Remember that you, in your consciousness, will be able to be transported to different levels of reality in an instant. This does not only mean the fourth and the fifth level. You will be able to travel to the different levels in the waking state, and not only in astral dream travel. Communication with elderly friends and learned ones will happen in a clearer and more conscious way, to open you up for higher knowledge. This prepares you for the next pyramid, which is precisely about higher knowledge.

Pyramid 6
The Book of Knowledge ... Sacred Scrolls

The sixth pyramid matrix is located over Tibet. Here the keys to spiritual higher knowledge are found, which you need now to open up for higher wisdom. This is the pyramid with the creation pattern that connects you to your spiritual wisdom and knowledge. This pyramid contains the knowledge that was brought from both Lemuria and Atlantis. As a scribe, it was my task to ensure that these teachings were registered through oral tradition, sacred texts, and scrolls. They have also been preserved in crystalline forms, in minerals and stone formations. Many have spread and preserved the knowledge through various channeled art forms, hieroglyphs, pictographs, and manuscripts.

We can call the frequencies here The Book of Knowledge, a temple for higher knowledge. It includes all forms of knowledge, not just higher spiritual knowledge, but also the sacred geometry that is the blueprint for all higher knowledge and all that exists. It is also within this pyramid matrix that spiritual teachings are created, based on the needs within each culture as it evolves.

The twelve priests and priestesses who brought the knowledge from Atlantis form the basis for the different cultures and peoples that have existed ever since the fall of Atlantis. These cultures, in turn, have created different systems that actually are parts of the wholeness. No system is erroneous, but they are all connected.

The Book of Knowledge means that all systems, peoples, civilizations, and units are merged into a wholeness. All that exists, all teachings, shall now surface and create The Book of Knowledge.

The frequencies from here have a strong connection to all pyramids, planetary systems, and the Milky Way. Many souls carry memories of coming to Earth as Tibetan monks through this particular pyramid. All higher spiritual leaders, priests, and priestesses, who have been on Earth through the ages, have been born into this frequency to acquire their knowledge. Through the ages, they have been allowed to keep the great sacred knowledge by being able to gather strength through this pyramid.

These Masters and leaders have preserved the knowledge until today, to pass it on in every civilization. It is in the frequencies of this pyramid that spiritual masters and teachers, angels, and spiritual guides have their base to work on Earth. It is written that these teachers have secret scrolls hidden away since the dawn of mankind. These teachings can now be found during the final stage of this cycle as keys, to open that which was closed and locked in. This is knowledge that you carry within you, that you brought down to Earth before your birth as a little child.

When you are to enter Earth in physical form, you plan and prepare what you want to achieve. You bring with you all the knowledge, but before birth to Earth, the access to it is sealed. It is more or less sealed in different people. You will now have access to it again through the keys of this pyramid. It is only after entrance to this pyramid that you will get the keys to eventually understand the wholeness fully.

Your guides, who you work with daily, are working through these frequencies. My hope is that those of you who do not have a daily contact and a clear communication with them will be able to open up for this through the frequencies of this pyramid.

To Visit Pyramid 6

When you enter the pyramid, have the purpose and the intention that you want to reach higher knowledge and wisdom. Enter this pyramid and ask your guides to meet you here for conversations.

The guardian of the pyramid, Tsu Li, will at some point during your visit hand over a papyrus scroll, a text with the knowledge that you need right now to move on in your spiritual development and reach a higher knowledge than what you possess at the moment. It is this scroll, these texts, that are your keys. Even though you cannot see this writing, it will be offered to you. Thus, have the intention to receive your keys to higher cosmic knowledge.

Open yourself for what and who you will meet, and do not worry if you meet an aspect of yourself, your twin aspect that carries all knowledge and turns it over to you.

Now step into this pyramid, where these teachings await you. Join with the three great powerful energies in this pyramid matrix, the frequencies from the three corners of the pyramid. Read their words in your papyrus scroll, and heed their messages. Then you will gain answers, knowledge, and wisdom.

Meditation Exercise 6

Close your eyes, relax, and feel that you find yourself outside the sacred Pyramid of Cheops.

See how you walk around it, until you find your own entrance.

Step into the base and follow the spiral of light up to the second chamber of sacred tones and light. Travel with it around and up.

Just feel how you become taller and taller in your light body.

Finally you slow down, step off, and stand in front of the door to the sacred Crystal Room.

Enter through the door, and find a place to sit.

Just feel how you calibrate yourself up, higher and higher in frequency.

My co-workers are now standing behind you and put their hands upon your shoulders and help you to rise in frequency.

Feel how the tones and the light go into every cell.

You have now been calibrated up to Pyramid 1, the etheric chamber of light and sound.

Now see how the ceiling is opened, or how a door is opened, and the sacred spiral appears.

Step into this spiral and follow it to Pyramid 6, the sacred temple in Tibet with the sacred mountains, the papyrus scrolls, the writings, and The Book of Knowledge.

Just feel how you become taller and taller, until you enter the base of this temple.

Step into the temple and Tsu Li will meet up with you.

Just follow her into the halls of knowledge and walk around there.

When you feel ready, leave the mountains and the temple.

Go back to the spiral that leads you to the second chamber in Pyramid 1.

Remember that you can return whenever you want.

Just follow the spiral in the opposite direction back, all the way to the second chamber in Pyramid 1.

Feel how you sit down in the Crystal Room and refill yourself with light and sound.

The prisms of the crystal emanate colors that go into every cell.

Feel how you are slowly calibrated down in frequency, until you sit in the second chamber of the Pyramid of Cheops.

Step out of the door and take the spiral down to the base.

Exit the pyramid and come back to the waking state.

It may happen that on each occasion you visit the pyramid, you will be assigned a papyrus scroll, a writing with different content and meaning. One cannot receive the whole key at once, but it must happen little by little, based on each person's level of knowledge.

Pyramid 7
The Dreamtime

Pyramid 7 is located over Australia. It deals with your dreams and includes all the dreams you have experienced and are experiencing. The soul who guards and preserves the Dream Kingdom and creates through this pyramid is the Dream Keeper. When you go to the place of your sleep time, you reach the pyramid frequency through the dream state and meet the Dream Keeper. Before you fall asleep, ask the Dream Keeper to show your destiny and to awaken your consciousness. Here you should pay attention to the symbols that you get in the dream. Start drawing them and remember what comes to you.

You will remember more and more important events and experiences that you are involved in on your nocturnal astral travels, visits, and trainings. In this place you are free, there are no ties either inside or outside the Matrix. You can travel wherever you want, to any place and world you want.

The knowledge in this pyramid is given in the form of symbols during dreamtime to those who are ready. Once the knowledge has been received, you can use it to transport yourself between different realities, create in dreamtime in order to manifest in the waking state, and choose to experience or relive different chosen events from your daily life. By reliving these situations, problems can be solved or prevented. Here you are free, and anything can happen.

Some will see this dreamtime as a truer reality, for it is just as real as anything else within the Matrix. During the transformation, you will notice that you more and more often remember and can realize your dreams. The need for sleep will look different in the new Golden Age of Light. Sleeping time will be shortened. What you have previously only experienced in your dreamtime, you will more and more be able to experience in the waking state and experience as the reality it actually is. In the waking state, you will then be able to process and get new stimuli into your lives. When you work with this pyramid, the key for the knowledge of your Higher Self is opened and it will be able to be stored on a conscious level, not only in your subconscious.

The aborigines from this place are one of the untouched civilizations that still today keep the hidden knowledge alive through their trust and conviction about their origin. Find a deeper understanding and insight into how this people live through the pyramid. You need to understand that everything is sacred, not only the Human Kingdom. See the lower Nature Kingdoms, the Mineral, Plant, and Animal Kingdoms as sacred. Appreciate and value everything in your path.

To Visit Pyramid 7

If you receive symbols, then write them down or draw them. They give you answers and may be in the shape of your key. You can ask the Dream Keeper his name. All who enter the pyramid might receive different names, even though they are on the same frequency. Pyramid 7 can be seen as the red mountain or the red earth temple, a red pyramid. It is very physical in its structure, like a mountain. Here you have the opportunity to meet the Dream Keeper, but also the humans who come from this place, the Nature People. The sacred race will open you up and give you the keys to higher understanding of the Nature Kingdoms, of thought, and of the importance of dreams when it comes to man's harmonization and future development.

Meditation Exercise 7

Close your eyes, relax, and feel how you find yourself outside the sacred Pyramid of Cheops.

See how you walk around it, until you find your own entrance.

Step into the base, and follow the spiral of light up to the second chamber.

Just feel how you step into the spiral of sacred light and sacred tones.

You travel with it around and up, and you become taller and taller in your light body.

You slow down and stand in front of the door to the sacred Crystal Room.

Enter through the door and find your place to sit down.

Just feel how you calibrate yourself up, higher and higher in frequency.

Feel how the tones and the lights enter every cell.

You have now been calibrated up to Pyramid 1, the etheric chamber of light and sound.

Now see how the ceiling is opened, or a door is opened, and the sacred spiral appears before you.

Just follow this spiral to the seventh pyramid.

Travel on with the spiral to the temple of the red mountain that holds your dreams.

Just feel how you become taller and taller, until you enter and stop at the base of the red pyramid.

Take in the fragrances here.

Enter barefooted and feel the ground and the earth underneath your feet.

Take in the colors and walk ahead on the earthen floor until you meet the Dream Keeper and the Nature People.

Follow along, relax, and explore the sacred kingdom of the Nature People.

Allow the Dream Keeper to accompany you through the halls in the temple of this people.

This civilization will give you answers and your key.

Receive and open up your mind, for everything is possible.

Now leave the red pyramid of dreams, and thank those that you have met.

If you feel ready, go back to the spiral that leads you to the second chamber in Pyramid 1.

Remember that you can come back whenever you like.

Just follow the spiral in the opposite direction back, all the way to the chamber of crystals and tones.

Just feel how you sit down in the Crystal Room and refill yourself with light and sound.

The prisms of the crystal refract the light into colors that go into every cell.

Feel how you slowly calibrate yourself down in frequency, until you sit in the second chamber of the Pyramid of Cheops.

Step out through the door and take the spiral in the opposite direction, down to the base. Step out of the spiral and the pyramid and come back to the waking state.

It is important that you start connecting with nature. By this I do not only mean to be out in nature. Merge your energy with nature—Mother Earth, the trees, the earth, and the plants. Just go out in nature and sit down in a suitable place. Have the intention to merge your frequency with nature's, the Nature People's, and their knowledge about the Earth and all it accommodates. This will benefit the knowledge you receive from this pyramid.

You will notice that you merge your energy with the Earth, that you become one with Mother Earth and have direct contact.

Practice the technique to go out from your heart and embrace nature (see Exercise 4, Part 3). In one single breath, you can communicate with plants, animals, and nature in a very simple way. Creating a link in this way will help you to open up your heart and send out light and love. You will then have light and love in return and a higher understanding and knowledge.

Pyramid 8
Extraterrestrial Contact

Pyramid 8 is located over Antarctica and is the main portal to the Matrices of other planetary systems and to the Earth's inner world, a place I call Aggannon. It is not only this place in the Matrix that is an entrance for other civilizations to get to Gaia. Every pyramid has an opening to the Cosmos and an opening to Mother Earth, but this is the central main site that is composed of an opening, a runway.

Pyramid 8 is a training place for you to go to, where you may take part of very advanced technology and higher knowledge from other civilizations. Knowledge that has not been usable on Earth since the time of Atlantis, but becomes useful in the fifth level. Draw and write down what you receive.

The soul that oversees this pyramid goes by the name of Xerthaneus. The function of this pyramid is to create and guide experiences linked to the comings and goings of extraterrestrial beings who have always been a part of the history of planet Earth. A story was created of a great spaceship, buried beneath a gigantic lion, who serves as a marker. Similar markers are created on every place in the heavens that are linked to the Matrix.

The tale tells that when the time is ripe and the ice melts, many crafts will become visible and many traces of extraterrestrial existences will be revealed. Many people will see, hear, and perceive this. Metallic chains have tied this place and made it difficult for certain civilizations to enter the third density level. Now these chains have been opened and made it easier for them to appear before you. Keep your eyes open!

In this pyramid exists only light and love. Here there is total balance between the cosmic energy and the Earth's inner energy. Here you can experience a pink shimmer, as the red earthly energy blends with the heavenly, to a perfect harmonious balance. Please ask for this balance and harmony to be portioned to Earth and its inhabitants who need to take part in this energy.

In Pyramid 8 you will find the base of information from other existences' different systems that have come to Earth through various times. There have been many from these far-away worlds that were once part of the history of your planet. Their journeys have been encoded into the pyramid matrix by Xerthaneus and his two assistants. They have all gotten through this frequency to assist in human evolution.

Many of you feel strong connections and bonds to certain places in the Universe. You who have experiences through this pyramid frequency come from Sirius, Nibiru, Orion, Lyra, the Pleiades, Mars, Andromeda, Arcturus, Vega, Venus, and Jupiter, among others. You came to Earth in great spaceships and interacted with those who lived here on the planet, both on and below the Earth's surface and in the waters.

Many of you do not belong to Tellus. You consist of a glorious mix of people, and many of you are directly descended from some of these places. You are created with the assistance of other existences. Since your memories are strongly genetically encoded to these other worlds, they sometimes remain as very strong memories, stronger than those from Earth. This explains the homesickness many humans feel.

When you reach this pyramid, you can find out about your own origin. You can also take part in societies of extraterrestrial civilizations and receive knowledge about how they live there, without hierarchy, power, and control. Societies where all inhabitants are equal.

To Visit Pyramid 8

Xerthaneus will guide you through this geometric pyramid matrix of snow and ice crystal, so that you can remember and return home if you want and need to.

If you travel inward into the Earth, you can come across forests, seas, and mountains. Here you find an inner core and sun, but you also have access to the outer Sun. The gravity here is reversed.

You who live with a strong homesickness, a feeling of unrest that is difficult to explain, have the opportunity through these frequencies to find peace and harmony in your soul again. Through this pyramid you also have the possibility of finding your soul mate and converge with him/her in many different worlds and forms. You will be reunited in joy.

Place your consciousness in this pyramid to experience and understand everything about extraterrestrial activities and your own experiences from other extraterrestrial forms. The highest cosmic council meets regularly in these frequencies in this place. If you are lucky, you might be allowed to attend such a meeting. Do not get stuck in the beautiful scenery you will be able to see on the large runway, but get closer inside to study the techniques and the technologies of these incredible crafts. Do not forget that this is a training place.

Meditation Exercise 8

Close your eyes, relax, and feel that you find yourself outside the sacred Pyramid of Cheops.

Walk around it until you find your own entrance.

Step into the base and follow the spiral of light and sound up to the second chamber.

You go with it, around and up.

Just feel how you become taller and taller in your light body, until you slow down and stand in front of the door to the sacred Crystal Room.

Enter the door and find a place to sit.

Just feel how you calibrate yourself up, higher and higher in frequency.

Feel how the tones and the lights enter every cell.

You have now been calibrated up to the first pyramid, the etheric chamber of light and sound.

Now see how the ceiling is opened, or a door is opened with the number 8 on it, and the sacred spiral appears in front of you.

Travel with the spiral onwards to Pyramid 8, Antarctica.

This temple of snow and ice crystal will embrace you.

Enjoy the beautiful interior, totally of ice and crystal.

See the furniture, the crystal chandeliers, and the beautiful play of light.

Xerthaneus will meet you and guide you through the halls of ice crystal and give you your key.

Ask to have the answers to the following questions: Who am I? Where is my place of abode in the Universe?

Maybe you will meet an extraterrestrial existence.

Maybe you will get the opportunity to go on a trip with an extraterrestrial craft.

Be open to anything that can happen.

Remember that you can come back whenever you want and how often you want.

Go back to the base of the ice temple and follow the spiral in the opposite direction, back all the way to the chamber of crystals and tones.

Just feel how you sit down in the Crystal Room and refill yourself with light and sound.

The prisms of the crystal refract the light into colors that go into every cell.

Feel how you slowly calibrate yourself down in frequency, until you sit in the second chamber of the Pyramid of Cheops again.

Step out through the door and take the spiral in the opposite direction, down to the base.

Step out of the spiral and the pyramid and come back to the waking state.

If you want to cooperate with other intelligent existences, you can work through this frequency. Visits from other times, eras, and existences happen through the portal of this pyramid. If only you knew what partners exist around you! Many of them have direct contact with other planetary systems the whole day and night.

A lot of wisdom and knowledge will be revealed, both from extraterrestrial systems and from the light beings that help you in your daily life. Eventually, you must realize and accept that you no longer can keep the lid on for the observations being made.

Pyramid 9
The Laws of Nature ... The Power of Thought ... The Meltdown

There exists a pyramid matrix above the Arctic, whose purpose is balancing the poles of the planet and the consciousness. Parts of the pyramid are now melting down and creating a shift on all levels.

This is an important grid, with a message about the power of thought and psychological, emotional, and physical healing. The special frequency of the Arctic binds the poles together and keeps the connection with the twelve planets, your physical body, and Prime Creator in place. Here the important energy connections between all planes and levels are maintained.

All thoughts create a pattern, both good and less good thoughts. The thought pattern gives rise to a creation on a higher level. This creation is then drawn down to lower and lower levels to become increasingly physical. Notice that you do not get the ability to create with thought "for free." You yourself must learn to create. Everything is created based on a thought. Neither will you automatically become wiser when you ascend to the fifth level. That is why it is important to already now start practicing your abilities. How to create is the information that lies hidden in the entire Matrix.

The guardian of this pyramid is known by the frequency of Sophia Hokhmat. Sophia creates a lot of knowledge flowing through the pyramid matrix of the daytime consciousness, where souls learn and experience. In the pyramid, you can study the natural laws of creation and then develop and preserve your abilities to understand and grasp what is occurring in your reality. For it is in Sophia's pyramid matrix that souls understand the relationship between all things and the connections between them. Prime Creator acts as a hub in the center of all of this, and it is the creative thought energy that gives life to the twelve pyramids and their creations, based on the sacred geometry.

Here you understand how a soul is created and how that soul can be manifested in many realities simultaneously, while the knowledge from each experience in the pyramid matrix can be utilized.

The function of the frequencies of this pyramid is to understand the laws of nature and to overcome them. Here you can reach the knowledge of and the ability to create with thought. It is here that you are given the opportunity to move and change energy.

Is there anyone who has managed to pull their arm through solid matter? I want you to pay attention to what I have spoken of before, the example when you hold two magnets against each other. These are drawn to or are repelled from each other, depending on how you turn them. Your goal is to change the polarization in matter, so that the poles are drawn to each other instead of repelling each other. This is the technique that we used when we created the pyramids and the technique to create matter through the use of tones and crystal. Energy transportation is also based on this technique, changed polarization.

To Visit Pyramid 9

The pyramid is a harmony of ice crystal and water. It is now time to visit the halls with the knowledge of the power of thought and the understanding of the relationship between all things. The pyramid is about to dissolve and melt down and can be experienced as jellylike. This temple of ice crystal, snow, and melted snow will embrace you.

Combine your mind and consciousness with the pyramid matrix to understand all things in your world. Within this pyramid you can create and access great wisdom by a mere thought, a thought that is linked to all other thoughts, which bind the souls and the wisdom together. In a nanosecond of your time you will access, understand, and learn all this information. Write down everything you receive, even that which you do not understand. It may be in a symbolic or emotional form that the information comes to teach you to create by thought.

164

Meditation Exercise 9

Close your eyes, relax, and feel that you find yourself outside the sacred Pyramid of Cheops.

Walk around it until you find your own entrance.

Step into the base and follow the spiral of light and sound up to the second chamber.

You go with it, around and up.

Just feel how you become taller and taller in your light body, until you slow down and stand in front of the door to the sacred Crystal Room.

Enter the door and find a place to sit down.

Just feel how you calibrate yourself up higher and higher in frequency.

Feel how the tones and the lights enter every cell.

You have now been calibrated up to the first pyramid, the etheric chamber of light and sound.

Now see how the ceiling is opened, or a door with the number 9 is opened, and the sacred spiral appears in front of you.

Go with the spiral on to the base of Pyramid 9, the Arctic.

You will enter a portal in the form of a waterfall when you step out of the spiral.

Feel how this waterfall purifies you on all planes and levels.

Feel how the water balances your poles, how you are harmonized right down to the cellular level.

Stand for a moment in the waterfall and just enjoy.

Hear the sounds, see the colors, and feel its healing jets on your body.

Now walk into the pyramid that keeps the secrets of the laws of nature in its halls.

Receive your key and turn it around to open up your heart and the forgotten power.

Ask to get back your memory and your knowledge from this pyramid matrix.

Ask to have an experience of yourself in an existence where you have been in your full power.

Go back to the base and the waterfall.

Pass through it and follow the spiral in the opposite direction, back all the way to the second chamber of the first pyramid, to the room of tones and colors.

Just feel how you sit down in the Crystal Room and refill yourself with light and sound. The prisms of the crystal refract the light into colors that go into every cell.

Feel how you slowly calibrate yourself down in frequency, until you sit in the second chamber of the Pyramid of Cheops.

Step out through the door and take the spiral in the opposite direction, down to the base.

Step out of the spiral and the pyramid and come back to the waking state.

When you open your keys, you will be able to use this pyramid frequency together with the power of Pyramid 1 to change the polarization and thereby develop the possibility to move energy, yourself, objects, and to overcome the power that keeps the Earth in check, the force of gravity. Understand what knowledge you have access to.

Pyramid 10
Emotions

The tenth pyramid is located over the Inca ruins of Machu Picchu in Peru and can be emotionally intense to enter if you haven't first purified yourself from blockages and negative emotions. This is the pyramid of emotions. The pattern of this pyramid is to keep the emotions flowing in formless waves of energy, which flow and change within you from moment to moment.

The pyramid matrix is linked to the Nazca lines, and these two create a readymade pattern of design, a primeval pattern for community building. This pattern has been used by the guardian of this pyramid to create realities and places for civilizations, so that they could come to this planet and experience emotions in a sluggish form. The emotions of the third density level are of low nature, but of high value for the growth of the soul. It is within this pyramid that *emotions in their lowest frequency are possible to experience in physical form.*

The guardian who creates through this pyramid goes by the frequency Lubileah. She speaks to the people of Earth about a time long ago when souls descended through her pyramid to feel and experience emotions, ranging from the lowest frequency to those of pure light energy. The souls got to experience torture and torment, love and compassion. They came to weave all these emotions into words, deeds, and great dramas in which they took part and acted.

Through the flow of this emotional matrix, great works in writing, painting, and music have always come into existence as a result of your emotional expressions.

You who have come through this pyramid matrix have chosen to experience and get to know the entire range of emotions. Many return through this frequency life after life, since the emotions have a strong ally in the ego, and this in turn lures you into power games with emotions at the helm.

In this pyramid frequency, you will place a high value on the purest light energy that is created and holds all emotions in balance. This frequency is connected with that which man calls Love and keeps the soul eternal. When you strive to reach the higher emotions, you also have to experience great suffering through the lower emotions. This leads to higher understanding, humility, and wisdom.

By visiting this emotional temple, you can now get answers to the riddles of creation. Here you will find your answers, but maybe not those that you expect.

To Visit Pyramid 10

When you reach the matrix of this pyramid, you will be met by the full power of all emotions that you have ever felt. You must be able to meet and deal with them, in order for them to be transformed into only Love. I often talk to you about emotions and of the importance of purifying and cleansing. It is important to have done this before you reach these frequencies. If you feel that you carry many negative emotions, then try to free yourself from these (for example, by working with the Line) before you enter this pyramid.

The Earth is the planet where one can experience emotions in a considerably more physical form than anywhere else in the Universe. This is important for the soul to have experienced, to be able to split its consciousness on many planes, existences, and levels at the same time. This also gives you the opportunity to walk in and out of all these existences, levels, and realities, whenever you want and as you wish.

When you enter, you will experience all the emotions at the same time within you and with an understanding far beyond what you can comprehend. The key here includes all emotions that you carry. When you experience and feel these all at the same time, you free yourselves from many of your fears. Eventually, you can only feel true Love, which is a fusion of all feelings in balance.

When you feel pure Love, you love yourself fully and see yourself as light and love, completely liberated from dark thoughts. Then you neither send out any negativity. When you can love your worst enemy, then you love yourselves, and you may experience true Love. There is only one beautiful feeling that makes you grow as individuals, and that is Love.

Now come with me to the Pyramid of Emotions. This white temple above the Inca ruins in Machu Picchu will show you the way to the only true feeling, Love. Do not let old fears blind you or prevent you from seeing the truth about who you are. I will show you how to find peace and balance in your soul, let go of all your fears, and at the same time embrace all your emotions.

Meditation Exercise 10

Close your eyes, relax, and feel that you find yourself outside the sacred Pyramid of Cheops.

Walk around it until you find your own entrance.

Step into the base and follow the spiral of light and sound up to the second chamber.

You go with it, around and up.

Just feel how you become taller and taller in your light body, until you slow down and stand in front of the door to the sacred Crystal Room.

Enter through the door and find a place to sit. Maybe you will meet me, the guardian, or someone else that you need to meet right now.

Just feel how you calibrate yourself up, higher and higher in frequency.

Feel how the tones and the lights go into every cell.

You have now been calibrated up to the first pyramid, the etheric chamber of light and sound.

Now see how the ceiling is being opened or a door with the number 10 opens, and the sacred spiral appears in front of you.

Travel with the spiral on to the base in Pyramid 10 in Peru.

Step into this white Sun temple, located right above the forgotten city of the Andes.

Feel the energies from this wonder and enjoy all the wonderful flowers and all fragrances.

Meet Lubileah, receive your key, and follow her through the temple of emotions, with halls and rooms created in all their forms.

You will experience emotions ranging from the lowest frequency to those of purest light energy.

Feel how Love finally embraces your heart.

Peace and balance fill your whole being and make you feel happiness and appreciation for everything you have in your life.

When you feel ready, go back to the base of the temple of emotions and follow the spiral in the opposite direction back, all the way to the second chamber of the first pyramid, the room of tones and colors.

Just feel how you sit down in the Crystal Room and refill yourself with light and sound. The prisms of the crystal refract the light into colors that go into every cell.

Feel how you slowly calibrate yourself down in frequency, until you sit in the second chamber of the Pyramid of Cheops.

Step out through the door and take the spiral in the opposite direction, down to the base.

Step out of the spiral and the pyramid and come back to the waking state.

When you have experienced all the emotions again, only the purest feeling will remain, Love. You will then have found inner balance, spiritual balance.

Pyramid 11
Synchronization

Pyramid 11 exists over Mesoamerica, and the energies of the Mayan culture are strongly associated with this pyramid. The pyramid is located above one of the physical pyramids and contains the pattern for Time and Synchronization. In this pyramid, you find the patterns for all symbols. The key to this pyramid gives you all the symbols that are in tune with the laws of creation. They are created and conveyed out through this pyramid frequency. You look at and use these geometric symbols regularly in your everyday life. When you study them, this affects your body physically, and you get in contact with the frequencies from the eleventh pyramid. The symbols here are also closely connected to Pyramid 1.

The guardian of the pyramid is Quetzalcoatl. In the large time cycle, he created encoded keys that were stored in the different patterns of the pyramids to guide souls into a higher consciousness. It is now time to collect your keys and unlock the information in each pyramid in order to learn and to pass on the knowledge of the changes that always happen at the end of a time cycle. When you have reached the end of this cycle and opened the keys of the Matrix, you are ready to receive knowledge from all the pyramids and creation stories. The keys of the pyramids are coordinated in time and create a wholeness of the human experience. During your dreamtime and in meditation, you attract those keys that are synchronized with the necessary experiences you need right now in order to mature.

To Visit Pyramid 11

Go now to the halls of this pyramid that lead you back to your natural state of being. You will recognize your keys of light, and they will open your soul and your consciousness. Here you will experience both the parts and the wholeness of all other pyramid experiences in the Matrix.

Your thoughts are involved and influence the frequencies here. Do not let them obstruct your way to receive all knowledge from all pyramids.

This temple above ancient physical pyramids will show you the way to the composite knowledge from all pyramids.

Meditation Exercise 11

Close your eyes, relax, and feel that you find yourself outside the sacred Pyramid of Cheops.

Walk around it until you find your own entrance.

Step into the base and follow the spiral of light and sound up to the second chamber.

You go with it, around and up.

Just feel how you become taller and taller in your light body, until you slow down and stand in front of the door to the sacred Crystal Room.

Enter the door and find a place to sit.

Just feel how you calibrate up, higher and higher in frequency, and how the tones and the lights go into every cell.

You have now been calibrated up to Pyramid 1.

Now see how the ceiling or a door with the number 11 opens, and the spiral appears.

Just follow this spiral around and around to the base in Pyramid 11, Mesoamerica and the Mayan culture.

Meet the guardian, receive the key of light, and follow him through the halls of the shining temple with the intention of finding a higher consciousness.

Maybe you will meet the Mayan people that will show you the way through this majestic pyramid and give you insights about the state of beingness from a time long past.

When you wander through the halls of the temple, you can perceive the other pyramids in different rooms.

Go into the hall that you feel drawn to.

When you feel ready, go back to the base of the Mayan pyramid and follow the spiral in the opposite direction, back all the way to the second chamber of the first pyramid, the room of tones and colors.

Just feel how you sit down in the Crystal Room and refill yourself with light and sound. The prisms of the crystals refract the light into wonderful colors that go into every cell of your body.

Feel how you slowly calibrate yourself down in frequency, until you are in the second chamber of the Pyramid of Cheops.

Step out through the door and take the spiral in the opposite direction, down to the base.

Step out of the spiral and the pyramid and come back to the waking state.

When you understand the entire Pyramid Matrix as a wholeness of a time cycle, you will find all the answers.

The eleventh pyramid unites all wisdom and knowledge. It is time to return to and wake up all ancient knowledge and experience from all earlier eras and civilizations. These old wise teachings and knowledge shall be used and utilized—the frequency patterns are of great importance and will merge into a new knowledge of life, and you "see the light in the tunnel" that leads you to the end of the story.

Pyramid 12
The Story Ends ...

The end of my story takes you to New York City and the twelfth pyramid. This pyramid has a somewhat smaller form than the other pyramids and contains knowledge about the journey home. Here are geometric symbols and patterns that guide you, including the bridge you pass on your way back home. Here is the pattern for ascension, just as the pattern for descension is in Pyramid 1.

This is the feminine pyramid, and the soul who oversees this pyramid goes by the frequency of Isis. She is the female aspect in everything that moves through the Pyramid Matrix. In other mythologies, she goes by the names of Sekhmet and Hathor. They are all one and the same energy frequency. She brings the Pyramid Matrix full circle, closing the circle.

It is Isis who expresses herself in the form of Mother Earth and is the creator of life and evolution. She weaves her creation into the fabric of time and sends her feminine energy to the Pyramid Matrix in order to maintain and balance the reality that you exist in.

She has no form, other than light. Her energies move through the creation of the Pyramid Matrix and flow through the consciousness of all that exists, has existed, and will exist.

This pyramid brings, as I said, the entire Matrix full circle, closing the circle. A new beginning took shape in 2001 with the tragic event of the Twin Towers in New York City that affected the whole world. This event became the start of the last cycle before the transformation and the new Golden Age of Light.

In this pyramid, you can follow all transitions that you have had in this and other lives. Here you learn about the circle of life. About all transitions in life and after life, how everything goes in cycles for an eternity. You get a deeper understanding and knowledge of how the circle, the cycle, and the Matrix work. The transitions are the end and the beginning of a cycle, from childhood to youth, from teenager to adult, from woman to mother, and from one life to another.

I have met many people who have difficulties with transitions in life. Often this originates in that they have had many difficult transitions where they suffered severe pain and great loss. This has created memories and fears that have not been processed and that they have brought with them to their next incarnation. It may involve an imprint that has been passed on for generations or a situation where someone is holding on to a dear person and is having difficulties in letting go. Also, in the case of mental confusion, the transition may be difficult, as with a sudden and unexpected death or when someone mentally has gotten stuck at an early age, although the body grows old and dies. When one stagnates mentally in this way, one is often not aware of it, but it lies in the unconscious. When all actions, thoughts, and emotions you send out come from a child's perspective, the ability to give love, tenderness, and care for oneself is lost. At a young age, you are still bound to someone else's care and love. You can work with all these phenomena through the frequencies of Pyramid 12.

To Visit Pyramid 12

Here you will be able to experience the transitions that you had during this earthly life, earlier existences, and future forms. Let the key open up for the knowledge about the journey home, the transformation, and the transition.

Find the geometric symbols and patterns that will guide you into the feminine age. This pyramid has halls in both modern and aged design. Concrete and glass is here mixed with architecture from times gone by.

Now step into the feminine pyramid created by the overtones from the Light of Creation, which now is returning to Earth.

Meditation Exercise 12

Close your eyes, relax, and feel that you find yourself outside the sacred Pyramid of Cheops.

Walk around until you find your own entrance.

Step into the base and follow the spiral of light and sound up to the second chamber.

You go with it, around and up.

Just feel how you become taller and taller in your light body, until you slow down and stand in front of the door to the sacred Crystal Room.

Enter through the door and find a place to sit.

Just feel how you calibrate up, higher and higher in frequency, and how the tones and lights go into every cell.

You have now been calibrated up to Pyramid 1.

Now see how the ceiling or a door with the number 12 is opening, and the sacred spiral appears in front of you.

Travel with the spiral to the base of Pyramid 12, the pyramid above New York City.

Meet Isis, Mother Earth, and feel into the feminine power and knowledge.

Receive your key. Follow along through the halls in this modern temple.

Walk in the halls of glass, steel, and concrete, and open up to everything that comes your way. Meet all the old and new. They are one and the same.

Listen, and you will get the answers.

When you feel ready, go back to the base of the pyramid and follow the spiral in the opposite direction, all the way back to the second chamber of the first pyramid, to the room of tones and colors.

Just feel how you sit down in the Crystal Room and refill yourself with light and sound.

The prisms of the crystals refract the light into colors that go into every cell.

Feel how you slowly calibrate yourself down in frequency, until you sit in the second chamber of the Pyramid of Cheops.

Step out through the door and take the spiral in the opposite direction down to the base.

Step out of the spiral and the pyramid and come back to the waking state.

When you reach the frequency of the twelfth pyramid, and all thirty-six frequencies are opened, the transformation will go easily and smoothly.

The transformation is your metamorphosis, your transition from the physical life you are used to, to life at a higher frequency with a higher consciousness.

When you have raised your consciousness via the twelve pyramids, you are transformed in and through the black hole in the center of the Milky Way. As I said in the beginning of the story, the black hole is the vacuum, the void that leads to another Universe, from where the twelve pyramids came. Here you are guided by the sacred spirals of geometry through this void. You have reached completion, and the transition to an existence on the fifth density level begins. You have started your journey home.

Each pyramid is a tale of its own within the tale. Work your way through the tales of the pyramids, and open yourself to the knowledge they help you to find.

Now my story has come to an end, and your journey continues. You can always reach me; call upon me whenever you want.

Goodbye for now, we will meet again.

Part 5

Questions and Answers

General Questions

I have a question about creating. I wonder if the same rules apply for creating when it comes to money as for other things. Is there an energy around money that makes it difficult to materialize it, or is there a darkness around money because it is linked to power?

There are no impediments in creating money. You can create anything you want, and it is true that you can create money. But then you have forgotten that I have explained that you should try to live non-materialistically in a material world, to open up your heart. If you instead focus on creating what you once planned would become your life's mission, then money will come automatically. You will get what you need.

If you understand the content of this book and start working with what it mediates, then you will create an energy around you that deeply affects and touches everyone you meet. They will in turn do the same thing to other people. These are the links of the chain that I've mentioned so many times. When you have achieved an energy field free of imprints and negativity, you will have endless opportunities, and the money you need will automatically be available. Money is something that you need right now, but which you eventually will not need.

The best creating is when you are so open that the thought energy comes out and is materialized immediately. Do you think that it took me ten years to build the Pyramid of Cheops? Not at all. It was manifested in an instant. It was transformed down from a higher frequency and was transformed into dense matter.

Everything is possible, my friends.

You say that everything happens now and that linear time does not exist. Why is it, then, that you use words like now and then?

I have to use those concepts of time; otherwise you will not understand what I am talking about. At the time of the fall of Atlantis, it was necessary to create the ability to think linearly. You closed your keys to the higher knowledge, and your level of consciousness fell. Linear time was created for you to get a grip on, and the context of, your lives on the third plane.

When the higher knowledge is opened again, you will understand what non-linear time means; you do not have to limit yourself. You will at any time be able to enter any of your existences. You say that you have lived different lives and have incarnated in different times. But everything happens here and now. All your existences are actually one and the same. Even if you sometimes can get a glimpse of yourself in ancient clothes, you also live that life here and now. You will discover common patterns and connections between the lives.

If everything exists here and now, you are in tune with and contemporary with the Big Bang and Prime Creator, aren't you? If you are linked to Prime Creator, then you realize what a fantastic power and potential you actually have. You just have to grasp that you can weigh the anchor at any time.

It is your brain that puts obstacles in your way. The day you get both your hemispheres in balance, you will discover that you use a very small part of the brain, just a few miserable percentages of its capacity. The goal is to be able to start using a larger part of it and to achieve harmony between your heart and brain. Today your consciousness is in your brain during most of the hours of the day, a brain that is not in harmony with the heart.

If it really was in Atlantis that linear time, light, and darkness were created, then I wonder why it happened?

It turned out that things weren't going particularly well in Atlantis. Humanity was forced to live on a lower frequency level than before, and that affected her. When we created new civilizations and human species all over the planet, we had to make the world around more understandable to them, in order for them to hold on to the physical form. For those who came from a non-material world, it was simply not possible to live without a framework in the material world.

Linear time makes it comprehensible for a physical brain to perceive a course of events as a chain of events. Light and darkness were created by the humans themselves. What you today term as light and

183

darkness is a descending transformation of the original balance, the yin and yang of duality. When yin and yang act in a dense world, the act of balance becomes harder, the power and the ego outweigh the reason and the compassion.

How many levels are there?

Different teachers have various opinions on this, but according to me there are twelve, with a thirteenth as the unity, the sum of them all. But you are welcome to believe anything you want. There are those who claim that there are seven, and a common opinion is that there are ten. It does not matter. Every plane and level has many sublevels, so it is a very broad spectrum of planes and levels we are talking about.

I wonder about the evil on Earth. Is it forces coming from outside or the personality of man that is the cause of this?

Evil is created by man. Pyramid 2 is about this. Most often it is the experience from misuse of power and different kinds of abuse that affect the behavior of man to turn into hatred. Everybody makes their own choices and how they choose to tackle difficulties in life. You choose if you want to be filled with hatred, lust for power, and other negative emotions in the void that is formed when the basic love is removed through negative experiences, especially in early child years.

Everyone is born good, but can get "incorrect" patterns by traumas in their lives. Man carries memories from all lives, and when one experiences a trauma, these earlier memories may be brought to life, something that can give rise to strong anger. Even the society can imprint evil in individuals. Sometimes less good energies might take over the human body, but this is very unusual, as this kind of phenomena has long since been cleared from Earth.

I have a question about evil on Earth and about the Norwegian man who shot many of the young people in a summer camp. Was there an agreement on a higher level between all the people involved? Or was it something that went wrong?

Interesting question you ask. There are many evil acts that have been perpetrated by humans on Earth, like for example by the Norwegian or the one called Hitler. Firstly, their acts naturally rebounded back on themselves. Secondly, they had a plan and a purpose for their actions, even though for your perception of reality, it feels inconceivable. Do you believe that the people who sacrificed their lives at this incident in Norway had decided this destiny before their birth? Nothing of what you call acts of evil has happened on Earth without a purpose. What happened after this massacre? A whole population *got to experience cooperation and love.* It was like ripples on water that spread on to a whole world, wasn't it? It sounds terrible, of course, when I say this, and the parents to the children who became victims would perhaps like to decapitate this body if they heard this. They would react, because of all the pain, sorrow, and anger that they feel. But remember that the agreement was made even with them, all the close relatives to the victims.

I have a supplementary question on this Norwegian event. If it really was an agreement before they came to Earth, and the event was triggered, were there no other possibilities? If the collective has another choice, then one does not need to stage such horrible things, right?

There are always many possibilities and choices. Some survived, did they not? Their time was not destined to end. But some of the lives were to end when they did; there was a meaning to it. If their lives had not ended there, maybe they would have drowned or have had another kind of accident or disease. So in this case there was an agreement, both for a higher purpose and also because their lives or their time were destined to end. I can discuss this with this body (Paula) for thousands of hours, and she never gives in. Of course, it must be a coincidence, she says, or why does the little child die, that cannot be the purpose, and so on. I insist, my friends, there are no coincidences; what happens in life is meant to happen. A human often has plenty of options to how and when she is going to leave the Earth. When she has fulfilled what was the main purpose of life, she turns back and goes home. If one does not fulfill anything of what was prearranged before birth, one has to go "home" at the first possible opportunity given. In that case, one has no more business to be on Earth.

What time bands are there between cause and effect?

Very interesting question, since time does not exist. You ask the "old man," who is least able to handle linear time. I can tell you that both cause and effect can be contained within a second, but that there also may be several lifetimes between them. Thus, you may experience cause and effect within a wink. But it may also be very long, according to linear time.

Will this change now in the New Age?

It is changing every day. The difference is that what you are thinking will come true much quicker, and it will go faster and faster. So give heed to your thoughts, my friend. Live life and play like a little child, and you will have wonderful gifts.

I have learned that the god and goddess of the Sun we see today are Helios and Vesta. Once I asked another psychic about the difference between Ra and Helios and then got the answer that Ra rules over a kingdom called Hexus, which I understand exists inside of the Earth, and that everybody knew this in the old days. So my first question is if you'd like to comment on the difference between Helios and Ra and the second is if you could tell me what Hexus is.

The difference between Helios and Ra is only the name. Just like me, Ra has also worked on Earth in many eras. He is a close and dear friend of mine. We have worked together for a long time. We go under different names in different cultures. You can drop this, it is the same energy. What was the next question?

Hexus, a kingdom.

I have to consult, because I have not heard the name of this kingdom before. I will check what I am allowed to say ...

Ra was my companion at the time of Atlantis, but even long before this era we walked together on Earth for long periods, even before humanity existed. It is quite possible that this name is something that is associated with that period, long before Atlantis and Lemuria. Ra is not only the god of the Sun, but has also been worshiped by man as a sun god. He has many sides to his character and he has been with me, creating the Matrix that I speak about. It is important that you understand that we, all the frequencies in the Matrix, cooperate on all levels. I cannot tell you more; maybe I can take the question with me and communicate with him to later on give you a more thorough answer to your question.

I have a question about the feminine aspect of Thoth and your consort, if you would like to comment on that.

I have chosen to keep her out of this, but I can tell you that she also goes under different names on Earth. My better half, I personally prefer to call Seshat.

Is she the same as Maat?

She has gone under many names and she is the better side of myself. I can inform all men of that. She was a scribe. Many of my texts would never have been able to be written down without my better half.

Can you describe the monad between Hermes, Buddha, and Thoth?

It is in many cases the same frequency range, but not the same soul. Thoth has walked through many times under other names. I have taken on other bodily shapes through the centuries and millennia. The three of them are separate souls, but from the same vibration. They are descended with different tasks, but with a similar ultimate objective.

I have a question concerning the Pyramid of Cheops. It was created in an instant, you say. I am thinking that those who lived nearby must have been very amazed and surprised that all of a sudden a pyramid was there.

Yes, I can tell you that the humans there were surprised when we came flying in something that we can call spaceships and landed among them. We had to master the indigenous people with the power of thought, so that they would not "mess" with us too much. We had to communicate with their highest leader, until they realized that it was very positive for their development. But certainly there was one here or there who fell to the ground.

Is this documented somewhere, and in that case, where?

It is preserved both in caves and in pyramids, both in Giza and in many other places in Egypt. If you look at cave paintings, you will in certain places see pictures of strange objects that fly.

Is there still hidden knowledge around the pyramids of Giza?

A lot of hidden knowledge is concealed and will come to the surface. Humans must first begin to understand this knowledge before it can be opened. There is no pyramid in the world that is older than the sacred Great Pyramid. It was built several thousand years earlier than what is commonly believed.

Are the pyramids that were found in Bosnia authentic?

Who said that these areas would not have pyramids? They are ancient, authentic, and powerful in their energies.

Excuse me, I have a question regarding this. Will more of those spaceships come here this year, so that history will be repeated?

It will be repeated, yes. It has repeated itself in all times here on Earth, more or less. Some in this hall have already seen them. The visitors will be visible more and more often. It is not really the visits that become more frequent, but the possibility to see them that is changed, as the frequency of the Earth increases. I guess you are aware that many things occur outside the registering ability of your eyes, that your physical body has controlled and limited what you have been able to see and not see. But then sometimes you get a glimpse of … what do you call it, the vehicles?

UFOs, Unidentified Flying Objects.

When you see these objects, it has sometimes been the case that they enter earthly frequency, that is, they are on a three-dimensional level. There are also some of you who can see them at the frequency of the fourth dimension. At certain periods there have been more observations, and they have been seen in many places at the same time. During other eras, it has been calmer.

You do not have to worry at all that the visitors coming here will have any evil intentions. The Earth is under very strong protection, and has been so for a long time past. You, who work day and night with clearing what you call negative entities and frequencies, have to understand that many of them have incurred you in another time, even though we live here and now. Time is not linear. Never forget that.

How and why did the Lemurian civilization end?

A very good question. We can partly thank the Atlanteans for this, as the Lemurians knew a couple of hundred years before—actually thousands of years before the fall of Atlantis—what would happen to this civilization. A few hundred years before the fall, they chose to leave their earthly form prematurely, to prevent facing the same destiny as the Atlanteans. Instead, they chose to raise themselves and their continent in frequency. This in order to form an example for humans to understand that they have a choice to make between living the tale that you are inside now and share the fate of Atlantis, or instead choose the Lemurian tale and raise your frequencies. It is two sides of the same coin. The Atlanteans also had this possibility, but out of their actions their egos grew big, too big to be able to take this path.

May I ask a question about kundalini and the snakes that wind around the so-called Mercury rod? Are the two channels that wind around the spinal canal actually the kundalini going upwards, whereas the divine power goes downwards? In that case, is the divine power going inside the spinal canal and the kundalini around it? Sometimes we are taught that one of the snakes around the rod goes upwards and the other one downwards. Could you clarify this a little bit?

It is not inside your spinal canal that the energies are flowing, but both of the powers, the divine and the earthly, flow through the two snakes. You are right about one of them symbolizing the divine power and the other one the Earth's power. But nothing says that they could not awaken and go into the spinal canal and spread upwards, although one is coming from above and the other one from below.

We have heard that it is not so good if it goes into the spinal cord.

It will happen automatically. The only thing you have to do is to awaken your thought that it is time to wake up the energy. It will then be formed and spread just the way it should inside of you.

I have heard before that it can be pretty serious to unleash these kundalini powers.

That is why it has to happen in several steps. You must not unleash the power in an uncontrolled manner so that it starts to rise too quickly to your head. It is through the meditative state, when you visit the Lemurian frequencies in Pyramid 5, that you will be able to start the kundalini power. Then the body is ready to start this flow before the coming raisings of frequency. But it will not happen overnight. It will take the time needed and go at a pace that you can cope with.

Remember that for each day that passes, you rise in frequency, just like Earth. But you should, of course, not ask the power to explode inside you, and so neither will occur. You can just go inside and ask for these energies to get started, and this is something that has already happened in many of you. Many of you already experience this as back pain.

It is a bit tough to have such severe backaches that you can hardly function. Is there anything we can do about it, so that we can function in our everyday chores?

Work a lot with the frequencies of the pyramids and ask to get help to release and heal the pains. The pains are just the first step for this area to start moving. They are the first sign. For each day it will rise a little bit, but ask for help to get rid of the pains.

Is there something that we should be cautious about regarding the kundalini power?

Yes, that it starts too fast. You yourself can control the balance by going inside and focusing on the elements and the power in your heart, and feel love for yourself and your fellow human beings. Have the intention that everything happens at the pace it should, and make yourself aware that it shall begin. Spend a lot of time on balancing your brain, because when you balance it, the fire will be able to flow freely and support the balance. You are balancing your brain by staying calm. Practice going into and out of different meditative states and levels by forcing the body to not enter the sleep stage, but to remain in the state between sleep and waking.

What is going on in my crown chakra all the time?

A lot of things are going on in all the chakras. Firstly, you let go of all blockages in them, but what will happen in the future is that you are going to center yourself, linking together your upper and lower chakras. You will all sense different chakra areas and feel how they merge with each other to unite in your heart. It is simply preparation for opening, purification, cleansing, and merging.

I have a question about the heart. I have learned that what we call the Higher Self on a certain level is a Trinity, and thereby the part of our spirit that incarnates is making it triune, threefold, namely in the solar plexus, in the heart, and in the brain. But I have also heard you say that the soul incarnates solely around the heart. Would you like to comment on that?

You are right about it being triune. Your religion bears witness to this; the triangle has three corners, doesn't it? Everything starts with three. The soul's habitation is between the heart and the pericardium, that is, the envelope around the heart. It is true.

Isn't the soul that is incarnated then divided and incarnated, with one part in the brain, one part in the heart, and one part in the solar plexus?

Partly you are right in that the soul is on all the three levels, but the power or the primary seed of your soul places itself in the heart. You forget the bodies on the outside that are directly linked to the main habitation of the soul. Certainly, parts of your soul are located in different places, but still the main location of the soul is in the heart. Everything has a link both downwards and upwards. Downwards to the solar plexus and on down to the base, and upwards to the brain, as you say, via the spinal cord, but also to other channels that I have spoken about. You can call them energy pathways or meridians.

You said that the people of Atlantis and Lemuria knew what would happen several centuries in advance. I feel that there is another kind of unconsciousness in humanity today. We have lived in the third density for so long that we perhaps are not that many who yet understand, know, and feel that changes are occurring. Do all humans change, even though they are unaware of what is going on or what will happen ahead? Can we do more than what we currently do to help our fellow human beings to wake up?

Choose to go out with the intention that everybody shall be affected by you. It does not need to occur verbally, but it can happen energetically from you. You who are conscious, try to open up others to become aware of what is happening. It can occur silently. It does not need to occur through the spoken word, since you all live together in the circles that I have spoken so much about.

Everybody will be allowed to follow if they choose this, but not everybody will want to. It is a conscious choice that you make, based on the inner insight that it will happen and thereby change your journey and your higher knowledge. Those of you who choose to follow, do this because you already, before you went into your physical body, have decided that it will be. Some will follow because that is what they have decided, but they are not aware that they took this decision before their birth. But always it so happens that they are close to fellow human beings who can help them to become conscious.

Remember that becoming conscious will happen in an instant, when all the keys are open. The work you put in is not always fair, but this is how the system works. Some help others, and this is one of your tasks here on Earth. Some have to work with themselves to purify and cleanse, whereas others, so to speak, just come along. I shall see if I find suitable words … to get a free ride. Do you understand what I mean?

Oh yes! Some have chosen to plod through deep snow, making tracks, while others just get a free ride.

Exactly! You who are in this room are making tracks in deep snow and doing the preparatory work, but above all, you do the great work of helping the Earth to manage these raisings of frequency. We from our side cannot do the work without help from humanity, and some are chosen for the mission to help us make this possible.

Everything will be how it was meant to be, the day the time has come. You will not have to worry about waking up sleeping powers that might hurt you, but it is important that you have worked with your lifelines before you get started. It is good to have done your purifications and cleansings, and you should have been inside the pyramids and worked a little bit in each one of them.

You speak a great deal about that one should work and enter the pyramids, as we have done so far. But for me it feels as if it goes by itself, and it does not feel as if I am working.

It does. Those of you who are conscious do not have to enter and exit the pyramids hundreds of times to get the work done. But you should enter all twelve at least once, to receive their respective keys. But it is as you say, the information goes automatically into the unconscious mind that stores it, as the Matrix is opened by me, together with the groups I am working with.

When the seven chakras of the physical body are to become three, will then also our DNA structure and cell structure be in tune with the change? Will it be harmonized or will it be noticeable?

For some who are sensitive to energy, it will be more and more noticeable. But please notice, this is a slow process. It isn't completed in your bodies until you cross over to the fifth level, and then it won't be so painful. But some who try to hurry or are very open will feel pain within certain chakra areas.

Where will these chakras be located?

Interesting question. Your physical bodies will change along the way, but there will be a somewhat lower chakra (however not as low as today), one in the heart, and one upper chakra. These chakras will be evened out somewhat and create a pyramid shape, a trinity.

Does this mean that the flows in the body connecting the chakras we currently have will also change?

Possibly, but not necessarily, because your physical bodies will change to become less physical. This means that the memories of your flows will remain, but you will not need to use these fully when you have crossed over into the fifth level. You will use new flows where you communicate in we-form, and then the flows will exist in harmonizing situations connected to others and not inside yourself. So new pathways will be created, but just as you have stored memories of earlier existences, you will have stored memories of your current bodies. You will not be in need of them in the same way. On the other hand, the outer chakras will be more important. Those that are not located inside of your physical body will link you all together.

If we now are going to enter the fourth dimension by the end of this year, how long is the time period to the fifth? It is, of course, a rather long transition.

It is difficult for me to predict the time aspect, but from the time the transformation started with the event in New York a certain number of years ago, how long ago is it in your present chronology?

Eleven years ago.

In that case you can expect that it will certainly take another ten to fifteen years until the entire transformation is completed. From the start, maybe twenty, or even twenty-five years, depending on how everything flows. Remember that I am bad at estimating linear time, but you will enter the fourth level quite low. During this period, you will slowly rise through the many different planes that exist only in the fourth level. In the beginning, you will hardly notice anything. Not more than that, I'm telling you to go out and play with energies, to open up to your inner knowledge.

Realize that you can and do have the ability to move energy, play with it, heal, and perform miracles. Begin using these abilities, and you will notice that it is true, as time passes, that things happen. When you send out a thought, it comes right back. When you work with healing, you can actually achieve healing on a deeper level than before. When you send out a negative thought (which you, of course, should not do), it will immediately bounce back to you in an even bigger form. Everything that you give is what you get in return. So start playing and moving things. See how you change polarity in objects and work a lot with yourself, but also with the Earth, when you are out in nature. Feel the pulsations of the Earth.

I sometimes experience that boundaries become blurred, that the edges of objects fade.

Welcome to the club. Welcome to how it is for me when I sit here in this body. Then you know that you are well on track. Just welcome it, and allow the boundaries to continue becoming blurred.

Those of you who enter a higher energy quicker than others will also discover that the boundaries of humans are becoming blurred and that you sometimes see objects unclearly. It feels as if you need to use glasses, like lenses before your eyes. Once Earth is ready and comes up to the first part of the fourth level, all humans will be transformed and start making their final choices. You also must accept that not everyone will make the same choices as you.

When we talk about frequencies, are we then talking about wavelike forms?

We talk about all kinds of frequencies. The patterns might look different. The wavelike is, among other things, the form that is falling down to the Earth's surface. The pyramids carry different forms of frequencies.

How bound is the soul to the body after birth?

195

The soul can leave the body in case of a severe physical disease. It wanders in and out of a baby's body, but takes, so to speak, place for a good ten days after the birth. In case of severe mental illness, it can partially leave the living human. The soul energy is then half outside the physical body and half inside the protective envelope of the heart. There are souls who have left the body, which then has been taken over by another soul, and exchanges of souls also exist. Such an exchange may occur during a heart transplant. In some respects, the medical developments can go too far. In Egypt and other ancient cultures, one knew this and treated the heart with respect. You can never take away the basic energy that belongs to the respective heart. Consequently, the impact for a heart transplanted person is great. Even though there is no exchange of souls, the person may be influenced by the basic energy of the new heart.

What is the mission of the soul?

The mission of your soul is to reach a higher level of consciousness. This means that you sometimes have to be exposed to less pleasant situations. Realize the purpose of every little occurrence in your lives. The one who performs negative actions must learn to live with the consequences of these. The Earth is unique, because of the strong feelings and the emotional life that can be experienced here, and that is why you often choose to redo life after life here. The experiences you have, and the strong feelings they evoke, help your souls to evolve.

If you are born with a special gift or knowledge, is it supposed to be used, or may it be the case that it is an imprint that should be removed?

Gifts are meant to be used for a higher purpose. If you are born with talents, they are meant to be used and developed, and not be wasted.

In what way will humans be born into the fifth dimension? How does it work? If we still do not die or there are not any bodies, then we would not have to be born into bodies either, would we?

Once we reach the fifth level, then death, as you know it today, will not exist.

But throughout the fourth level, death and birth will exist?
Exactly.

If I live until the age of ninety-four, then …
If you die before we have completed the transition, you will just choose to return here after you have crossed over into non-physical form. It is as simple as that. You will at any moment be able to pass any level you want, just the way you can using the keys in Pyramid 5. If you want to enter the earthly frequencies, which will then be on the fifth level (notice that this is a level that still will develop you), you can choose to enter this frequency whenever you want. Who said that you have to be born as small children? You will, when you cross over into the fifth level, be higher, more subtle, in your form. Then you do not have to begin from childhood and develop into adulthood.

What about old age?
No, when you are finished with what you need to develop, you go back to where you want to go.

But if I live until I am 95 years old, then I will live into the fifth dimension. Don't I have to die from my body, then?
You ask interesting questions. Some people will leave life on Earth, and some will be able to be transformed back to the age they feel that they want to be in.

What are the criteria for that choice?
We will get there when we are getting closer. You are a little bit too early.

We have a rather large chemical pollution of the environment going on, that affects the human body a lot. Can we, who are here, do something to ease the effect that happens today with our children?

197

You can work with all forms of chemicals in etheric form, and you have already mastered and received the keys and the knowledge to go in and do it. You can purify and cleanse your own and others' bodies on a higher vibratory level than what you understand. This means that you have to connect into the toxin of the substance. You ask to connect to the frequency of the substance. Then choose to reprogram its frequency into sacred energy from Prime Creator, so that you purify the frequency. This applies to all food that you eat. You should purify everything. Your physical bodies are purified gradually, but you can speed up and assist to transform away toxins energetically. Just like I mentioned earlier, that you should work with healing in your bodies outside the physical body to remove the memories, in the same way you remove the memories in toxins and things that you do not need.

A simpler version of this is to use kinesiology to find out the frequency of the toxin, to extinguish it. Does it work?

It works well, but this is so simple that no human needs to use complicated systems to find the right frequency. You have the knowledge that you have now opened with the key, so all you need to do to work with a frequency on a higher level is to connect with it. You do not need to complicate matters by visiting someone who can measure Hertz or something similar. You just think the thought, and you will be able to complete what you do. Connect your heart, if needed, to the frequency of the toxin, and ask to fill it with love and light. Many people have the ability to complicate things for themselves, because they have always had masters around them who have wanted to enlarge, change, and raise their egos by letting ordinary people feel small. They have reduced you in order to magnify themselves.

If one has a strong Christian faith and a belief in eternal life, but that this consists of rest and sleep, will one be in this sleep when crossing over?

Of course, there are individuals who do not grasp what I am talking about; they will be offered to see what it is all about one day, and then make their choices. This is what I was talking about earlier, that some get a free ride, while others do the heavy work. Such a sleeping person as you asked about then gets the opportunity to come along when it is time. Remember not to involve the religions in what we are talking about. The religions have always been and will always be a good way for man to maintain trust and belief that life does exist after the earthly life, even though it might not be the same philosophy that I convey to you here today. Remember what I told you earlier, that man during his existences here on Earth, and especially during this incarnation, has lost his trust in himself, his belief, and his Higher Self. This means that you are firmly anchored in the Earth, but have lost your higher communication, your higher contact. Others do exactly the opposite. They are out fluttering in the Cosmos and do not live as humans, which is just as devastating. This is why you should be humans and nothing else.

I have heard that at the time of Earth's transformation, there will be three days when you should turn inwards towards your own light. Will this occur at the transition to the fifth dimension, or earlier?

I know exactly what you are talking about. I am not entirely sure that there will be a blackout, but there is a possibility for it. The blackout would mean that the magnetism is changed and that there will be a weakening. This will not necessarily lead to a fast pole shift; it is not decided. Some talk about this in connection with the magnetism being weakened, and you know that the poles may change places then. It can occur within an hour back and forth, or take three days. In that case, a blackout would occur. If that occurs, it is certainly about finding the light within yourself, but also about having prepared yourself for this. If I have my way, I do not want any catastrophes. I want to do everything possible to minimize these, even though I might not succeed completely.

I usually have problems falling asleep. I have met you quite a few times now, and after each time I always fall asleep very easily. Even today I have had many flash naps.

Many people become affected in their physical bodies by what is happening. In your case, it is the sleep that becomes affected. When I come with my energies and frequencies, I work with each one of you in the room, including you. You are affected by my frequencies, and this makes your body, which actually needs sleep, end up in it, and your brainwaves go down to delta level. Remember that the frequencies of these brainwaves will change as you are raised in frequency. I am able to work on totally different levels than the five that we have talked about, and I do not end up in sleep, although the body is in sleep. If you measure the brainwaves in this body where I am, they would be in very low frequencies within the delta spectrum. We possibly speak about frequencies as low as 0.2 or 0.3 Hz.

We talked about that we should balance our brains. There is a system that a brain researcher has developed called Bars. It is about points and lines that you press on top of your head. Could this be helpful, or is it still so that we help ourselves best?

It is possible that it might help. All kinds of massage stimulate the flow of the energies.

The physical experience of the treatment is that you float out, and the thoughts that you had earlier do not take hold any more, but one gets a sense of calm and tranquility in a totally different way.

I know that the body (Paula) has been in many different meditations and had many different kinds of massage. They are all good and help the brain to calm down, as you say. At the same time, you also have to be able to increase the flow and go in the other direction, not just calm it down. All waves are of importance. I believe that this system works excellently as a help in the balancing, but it does not preclude that you yourself consciously must learn to master the different systems. But of course, it can help one to reach relaxation if she is stressed and needs to calm down. I am convinced that some new pathways are created between the right and the left hemispheres through similar kinds of stimuli.

Have I understood it correctly that our incarnation cycle will end with

200

this shift? That we no longer will come here in different forms and under various circumstances?

Partly you are right, to be sure, but partly not. You will continue to live. Many want to continue living on Earth in the new frequency. This does not mean that they are stuck on Earth, but that they will be able to choose to periodically leave the planet to go home. It is exactly the same as today, but with the difference that you do not need to start all over again each time as small children, who have forgotten the information about their former lives and who can be hampered in their development through external influence. You do not have to adapt, to live someone else's life, but you can live your own life. You can make the choices you yourselves want, and prepare and leave when you want to.

For a long time, even before the existence of Lemuria, I chose to go down to the body that had been formed and that would become Gaia, your Earth. I chose to harmonize energies and balance myself, but also the newly formed body, for a long, long time. This was a matter of many hundred thousand years. Then I myself chose to leave, which means that I partly learned to master death by escaping rebirth. You will also escape this. You have, of course, always been immortal, but you have understood it differently, because you have always left your physical body, meaning the shell.

Did you say that you incarnated on Earth, or did I misunderstand you?

I was on Earth at an early stage, yes.

As a human on that occasion?

No, not in human form. It was very hot, and very problematic to be in human form. I have been dormant for hundreds of thousands of years. I thought I had mentioned that. When you sit contained in the darkness, then you find the light. Just like I did, even though it took 250,000 years or so. It was after that I could master, I cannot say the laws of nature, because they were not created then, but I could master transformation on all levels. That is why people mention that a blackout may happen. This is, of course, all about development. If I have my

201

way, I do not want a blackout. But I cannot help if it happens. I will not be able to affect it.

A lot of information circulates about what will happen. Some say this and others say that. Depending on what we believe, can our mass consciousness become affected by this sometimes distorted information that is circulating?

That is correct. Your mass consciousness becomes stronger and stronger. The more who twist your mind around, the more misery can be created. More misery than what is needed. If I had my way, the transformation would only be such as night becomes day and day becomes night, without consequences. However, now I am not authorized to control this course. But what you say is totally correct. That is why we work on many planes and also need help from physical humans who can help us change things and send out accurate images.

Remember that whatever you read, whatever you hear, and whoever you listen to, whether it is me, a book, or any other source, you should only take in what feels right in your heart. Never, ever try to take in something just because someone else says it is good. If you follow your inner conviction and your inner voice, you will be guided properly. Remember that there is a universal truth. There are many who speak about the same things, but the mediating can occur in different ways and be interpreted differently. Everything I have talked about in this room has been interpreted in at least twenty different ways, if you are now twenty people in this room.

During the meditation, I met energies who told me to paint life. Paint with words. What does that mean?

Well, paint life, then. What is life for you?

I guess it is to be able to be here and now.

Are you here and now?

Not always.

No, but as much as you can, that is good. What do you think happens to your surroundings if they meet you and you are here and now?

You awaken a seed in others, so that they also can be here and now. You affect so many. When you have affected one individual, then the whole group eventually becomes affected. This in turn affects the Universe, and the Universe affects individuals. It is like a wheel of eternity. But open yourself and try to be for increasingly longer periods in joy and in your heart, and don't take on the energies of others. You, and nobody else, can take command over your life. It is only you who can decide which path you shall follow to get to the main road. So for all of you who like to blame others or various circumstances, let go of this and begin to realize your own responsibility for everything around you.

I guess there are more people than myself who have not been inside all the pyramids. I have missed number three.

No problem, you can enter and exit whenever you want. Every month another one is opened, both by me and by groups. You open and enter, and each time you enter you can open a small piece with the key you have received. When month twelve is over in the year 2012, all keys will be available for everyone. The only one who can limit you and your ability to use them is yourself and your trust. Your ego and your unconscious self can stop your higher consciousness from getting in full bloom.

There is a room below ground level in the Pyramid of Cheops. Can you say something briefly about this room?

There are many rooms that are known, but also those that only a few have knowledge of. The room below ground level is very sacred, because it leads down to subterranean worlds. It follows the energy tube that goes through the North and South Poles and into the center of the Earth. There are civilizations that I am not allowed to speak about yet, but who are very close to Atlantis. Remember that the Pyramid of Cheops was built as result of the fall of Atlantis. It was once located in Atlantis and was created there. When Atlantis fell, we recreated the pyramid in a new location that was carefully chosen. It was done both with energetic precision and with another higher purpose. The entire pyramid hides very important information. Please go down there in a meditative state. Go deeper and see what you find. Perhaps you are the chosen one who will step through. I am not allowed to say more than this. If you take a side road, you will automatically come to the Sphinx. A little advice you can use.

I would like to ask if Thoth has several channels.

I have many channels, and I visit a lot of humans and try to communicate with as many as possible. It is only in this body that I can enter this deeply right now, but I communicate with five Earth humans who take down my words in writing. But I am at the same time with thousands of humans and communicate.

When you understand your potential and your knowledge and begin to open the frequencies of the twelve pyramids with the keys, you will also realize that you are divisible, and just like me, you are in many places simultaneously. This is also something that I again want to clarify for all of you. You humans have so much knowledge, but there are so many of you who, due to adaptation, do not live according to your inner truth. But it is important to practice what one teaches and to have the courage to say no to such things that do not feel right in your soul, in your heart.

At an earlier visit in one of the pyramids, a lot of sorrow surfaced for me, and it felt as if it was not my own.

Remember that you carry with you sorrow from many existences, my friend, not only from this earthly life. So the connection you got when you entered the pyramid was sorrow from other existences that has been transformed down in memory form into your cells. That is why you did not experience it as your own.

I had a vision of a breathing exercise that looks like a standing number 8, when I was inside the pyramid. In the breathing, the number 8 changed to become a transversal 8 that was flowing through the entire system, but lying down instead.

It is fantastic how brilliant you are in this room, how you can create images in your mind's eye that help you with exactly what I have been talking about today. A transversal number 8 that flows through your body, a symbol of eternity that unites Yin and Yang, Heaven and Earth, and your inner system.

I would like to ask for a good way to remind oneself of this knowledge in daily life.

I'll try to find an example ... You constantly have to remind yourself, just like you say, for a change to occur. Can you put an alarm clock on alarm once every hour? No, I was just joking with you *(laughs)*. Can you tie a ribbon on the tip of your nose, perhaps? I cannot give more advice than telling you that you have to make yourself aware of this and every day create your own routines in your daily life, by giving yourself encouraging words, love, and refilling with light. Each one of you has to find your own way, but above all, become aware of when the great emotional aspects make their presence felt—anger, tears, and so on. Just let it come out and do not let it affect you anymore, and then just refill yourself with light.

Young people who are not feeling well today—should one bring them up with stricter rules or release one's hold when they go astray? It is so difficult to bring them up in the society of today.

That is correct. It is, of course, so, that the children who were born and are in their youth today are pre-programmed for a higher frequency. They find themselves in a far too slow frequency right now. This creates imbalance, and many of them get so-called letter diagnoses. Their behavior is not in accordance with what is desirable. Often these young people have behavior that is inappropriate, but which is actually natural for them, since they are on a higher frequency level already from the beginning. It is about responding to them with grace and starting to communicate with them about higher things. Talk to them about life, and why one lives. That is why many children and also young people have many questions, thoughts, and reflections that they cannot give expression to. These young people need to meet humans who can understand them, see them, and give them tools to bring out the higher consciousness that they carry. Gather a group, so I get to meet them. It is also about children who do not find their way, but wander about on side paths because they have adapted incorrectly to what they initially were descended to do. The children sense stronger frequencies than those that are here right now. I can also swear that everyone in this room the last months has had more palpitations, sleep disorders, or problems with pains in the physical body than they had before. This is a direct result of the body not physically following the raising of frequency. That is why relaxation and meditation are so important.

Which laws of nature are the strongest right now, and will these change?

There are many laws of nature, but as we go up into a higher frequency, some of these will indirectly slowly fade away. The law of cause and effect is still very strong and operates by the principle that what you send out, you also get in return. It is a law of nature that we have to use in the right way to not get negativity in return. Our sense of being separated from each other is still very strong, but this will, as we rise in frequency, change from a sense of I to a sense of communion. There are many laws that are about to end, but others that will continue to exist. The electromagnetic field around the Earth will become weaker.

You have probably heard that the possibility exists for a pole shift, that is, where the poles change places. It has happened before on several occasions during the Earth's existence. I cannot prophesy whether it will happen, because we have a pyramid that is trying to keep the system in place, in order for it to have the least possible impact on you humans. But in that the electromagnetic field is weakening, part of the laws of nature you have will also weaken or be abolished.

Why was the Sphinx built?

When a sacred place is to be built, it also needs to have a sacred guardian. The Sphinx guards the sacred pyramid and contains great forces, holy scripts, secret messages, and strong frequencies.

Were they built at the same time?

No, the Sphinx was built later. But that was because humanity had entered a time with a lot of trouble and disorder. A guardian was needed at the time, because humanity was then characterized by a lot of superstition. The Sphinx actually scared the physical humans. It guards, but accordingly, it was built later, when there was a need for it. Therefore I have, of course, been able to be involved and influence also this construction and leaked in knowledge into it, but I cannot tell you more than that. But it is important, very important for all humanity. It includes a lot of frequencies from me. In this way the area is guarded, and I am involved.

What about the other two pyramids located in the same place?

Yes, they were, of course, built in a somewhat later stage, but also earlier than what humanity believes. There are several rather small pyramids that I have not been involved with at all, but the other two big ones I have been involved in.

What is the function of the other two?

It is, among other things, about certain times of the year, when the planets and the solar system are in a specific position, which affects the energy in this area, and this in turn affects humanity. They also have a protective function for certain energies and secret knowledge.

All pyramids and the entire area carry hidden knowledge that we are now working to bring to light. Some of it is buried, other knowledge has followed living humans into death and has to be renewed the way we do today. The area has a protective, but also a strengthening function, for Earth. You can call it a power site that holds the energies on Earth. The astrology affects the site.

The humans who used the Pyramid of Cheops were able to use it as a time indicator, as the light from the Sun made it possible to use it as a clock. The light entered into the innermost sacred chamber a certain time of the day, when the Sun was at its highest point. So there is a reason why it stands where it stands.

There is an opening in this area that leads straight up through the etheric pyramid, through the planetary system, and up to Prime Creator. This connection makes it easy for spirit beings to get in. There are energy tunnels, pathways all over the Earth, that can be used both by the spirit world, by yourselves, and by other extraterrestrial existences. Sacred frequencies get through these pathways and affect the Earth's energy. They often show themselves as geometric patterns and formations in the cornfields. Please pay attention to these formations, as they affect you in the form of messages, both energetically and mentally.

I wonder about the relation between this pyramid grid and the power sites of the Earth, the Earth's grid.

There is a very strong relation, because the frequencies must be transferred down to the Earth's crust via something one could call cords or pathways with higher frequency, and of course, via you humans. So the power sites are of importance, but remember that many of them are not true power sites, but only memories, memories of ceremonies. They get their power from magic originating from the ceremonies that have taken place on these sites over the centuries and millennia. Those are not the true power sites.

On the other hand, the Earth's chakra system, with connections up to the Pyramid of Cheops and the area around it, is a true power site on Earth. So also are the Nazca Lines and others. There are some really big power sites and others that are smaller. But there are also many that are worshiped by humans and which are powerful because of their energy, but that do not have any further connection.

I wonder, as the chakra points of the Earth have moved, how does this affect these power sites on Earth? I am now thinking of supporting and helping the Earth in this transformation. Is the entire grid affected, and do the ancient power sites remain in the same positions, or do they also move?

Many old power sites still remain, that is why there are side paths, but many follow, just as you say. One could say that this grid partly protects, but it is changeable and moveable. The pyramids themselves

208

have almost all of them from the beginning been in the same location as they are in now. The exceptions are two that have changed position slightly. Between the pyramids, new pyramids are created in somewhat smaller etheric form, so the entire surface of the Earth is covered with this grid. In this grid, one will be able to move in the pathways we mentioned earlier. You do not know the position of one of the pyramids, and this is because it is not currently located where you think it is. It was created a very long time ago. Much has changed, and things look different now. Just live in the knowledge that what you call the Atlantic Ocean today perhaps has been called something else before.

May I then ask concerning planet X and magnetism and so on, will Planet X get so close to Earth that we will be affected?
   You are already affected.

But even more?
   The influence will be stronger, yes, but I cannot tell you anything about the consequences, about how weak the magnetism around the Earth will be, and if it will affect you in the way you refer to.

There are boxes, metallic boxes, that are placed along the coastlines and along the fault lines that are not earthly, so to speak. From what I understand, they hold back the movements of Mother Earth, so that we will get more time to prepare ourselves for what is to come. Is this true?
   I can tell you that this is nothing new, but that help has been lowered down at all times. There was a mistake this time, when they became visible. This is because the Earth has gone up in frequency, and you now can see such things that earlier were "invisible." It is true that you are getting help, both from us and from other civilizations. There are humans—I call them humans, although they do not look like you—from other civilizations who have strong "bonds of karma" to you and who assist. A downfall would be disastrous, because it affects the entire system. I cannot tell you more than that, but the information you have taken note of is correct.

It is said that there are channels inside the Pyramid of Cheops, one from the Queen's chamber that points towards the Pleiades and one from the King's chamber that points towards the Sirian system, or was it the other way around? Sometimes I can feel that I would like to experience my Pleiadean self closer, and thus the question is whether one can use these channels for more direct contact.

Of course, my friend, you can have direct contact with all the civilizations that you are drawn to.

Is it a good idea or not? This is an important question.

For you, my friend, the strongest for you is of course the Pleiades, but also Sirius. You already have contact, but if you want to be aware of this contact, it may be beneficial for you. You can get answers to questions you ponder about your origin. You can use the channels, but you can also use the pyramid of Antarctica.

Is it a good idea to bring down the Pyramid energy to certain locations to help the Earth?

Very nice, very good! Put this energy around yourself as a protection, and put it in locations for protection. Heal the Earth every morning or every day in meditative form. When you are doing this, talk positively to yourself. Give yourself commands every morning, and also include the Earth in this for healing and purification.

Is there any particular pyramid that is essential in this?

You will become aware that all of them have their part in this and play their role. But the one we have been inside now (Pyramid 2) is much about healing, so feel free to use this one. You can also use the crystals in Pyramid 1 or utilize the other pyramids in different ways.

I have a question about a planet that has been spotted that has started to become visible, since it has no physical matter.

Why do you think I have waited a bit to talk about all twelve planets? It is the twin planet of the Earth that you see, and it has been

210

located right behind the Sun. On the other side, we have not been able to observe it, but now we have been thrown around a little in the constellation around the Sun, because planet X has entered the solar system.

So it is actually true that it is our twin planet?
It is your twin planet.

Is there no name on it more than that?
You are welcome to create a name. We call it Tellus, just like the Earth. You can call it Twin, or whatever you want. When you were children, how many times did you say then, "Of course we are not alone in the Universe!" At some point when you grew older you lost the knowledge of the child, you forgot the feeling of not being alone. But the little child was right; you are not alone in the Milky Way Galaxy. It is only your science that hasn't realized that yet.

But then how come they erase and modify pictures at NASA? Is it still a matter of covering up, so that we will not be so afraid?
Do you remember ray number one? It can be misused, as well as being positive. It is about power and control. It is a long time since man was free. Both you and I say that you are born with free will, but if we are to take it one step further, it is a long time ago since man in creation was free. It is not even certain that you as a soul have ever lived a life when you have been totally free.

At some point, we must have been free, weren't we?
Yes, between your earthly lives, I guess you understand that you are free and at home, but I talk about free will in the form of existence that you are in now here on Earth. It is because power and madness in the frequencies, which also have included the pyramid you have been in today, have affected humanity and made her dangerous to others.

We can always call the twin planet of the Earth Htrae, it is Earth spelled backwards.

211

Very nice. Didn't I tell you that you would give it a name?

Is the twin of the Earth on about the same evolutionary level as we are?
This is what they will soon discover, if they have not already done so: that it is approximately at the same distance from the Sun as the Earth. It is of somewhat larger size, but I don't know what they have been able to measure yet. This is all I can say, but it is at approximately the same distance, yes. Now they are putting a muzzle on me, my co-workers.

Will the Earth goddess Gaia leave the soul and spirit for the new planet?
Gaia will not leave the Earth, but she will go through a cell division. What is happening right now is similar to the creation of the Earth, the Big Bang, or the creation of a human being with cell division, or like a drop from Prime Creator that divides itself and spreads.

Will it be 2.78 times larger in size than Earth?
Its area will be larger, yes.

Will there be another Sun, which is being formed?
I cannot confirm this information, but I can inform you that everything that happens will happen in the form of division.

While speaking about the planets and the Moon, I wonder why we react so strongly when it is full moon. What is happening?
Actually, it is at different times that the frequencies from the Moon affect you the most. That is why I, in addition to the twelve planets, can use it as a body in my teachings to you, because it affects man so strongly. Even though the Moon actually belongs to the fundamental frequency of the Earth, do you understand me? But it affects you the strongest during certain hours of the day or the month, and this is what you sense. But when you calibrate yourself and go up in frequency, it will affect you less and less. You are affected by all the phases of the Moon, but at full moon you feel the energies extra strongly and actually get the same symptoms as today when you are on your way up in

frequency. You might get nausea, headache, sleep disorders, and so on, much like a depression.

It could easily be interpreted as something negative.

It's just that when your body cannot receive these frequencies, it affects the physical body negatively. If you calibrate your frequency with the Moon's and you prepare your body in advance, you will not experience any physical symptoms. Of course, the Moon radiates more power towards our atmosphere and the Earth's surface when it is full than when the Sun only illuminates it partially.

There has been a great deal of activity in England lately, with UFO observations that were filmed during the first weeks of February. I wonder if you could say something about this.

I cannot say anything, unfortunately. It is not my task to talk about this with you, other than to point out that such observations will be more and more common. It is an increasing activity. They are here to help you in the position you are in. But it is also about old knowledge that will come to the surface and about humanity having to open their eyes and stop following a power and authority that wants to lead them into the future.

You are now the ones who are going to take command of your lives and live in a "we group," and with this, all truths have to come forth. That is why the visitors can be observed, and more similar events will be filmed. Finally, when these films can no longer be refuted, you might get some leaders over to your side. The authorities then have to ease the pressure and realize that they cannot protect you any more on a national level.

Do we actually need less sleep now? What can we do to have this deep rest at night, when there are such strong energies circulating?

You need less sleep now, but you have to make use of it. Even though you cannot sleep at night, you still have to rest, do you understand me, staying in bed squirming. Tell the body (Paula) who has had sleeping problems for many weeks, that she still gets the rest she needs. She has been worried that it might be due to stress or something similar, but it is actually the frequencies that affect your sleep, just like you say.

If you feel exhausted when you wake up, have you still gotten that rest?

Maybe not enough or completely. Wait an hour or so after you get out of bed and see if it works, otherwise you may begin lying down for a short moment sometime during the day to recover a little. Just lie down for short moments and breathe many deep breaths. Pay attention to your diet, eat less and healthier. Purify and bless your food and drink at each meal and give it the thirty-six frequencies. You might have to add some micro breaks until you have adjusted. Go into the Crystal Room in the Pyramid of Cheops. Five minutes is enough. You cannot overdose your visits there.

I find it difficult to purify and cleanse myself; it is stuck. It is difficult for me to forgive.

Instead of doing this during meditation, write down the emotions that hinder you on a piece of paper. Ask yourself questions like "Why do I feel this way? Why is it difficult for me to forgive?" You have a strong need to control, which is not yours. You have to accept and let go of this and begin to look upon every day as a new day. Ask yourself concrete questions and then burn the paper. Refill yourself with light and sound from Pyramid 1. If one cannot work with oneself, one should ask for help from the outside. The goal is to live in balance and harmony. Life does not have to be a hardship.

I have problems with energies coming in stopping my contact.

Are you aware that you are like a magnet? How often to you turn off your contact?

I never do.

You have to land and only be human, here and now, between the occasions when you work with energy. Put the lid on, and then open

214

consciously when it is time for communication. If you are distracted, are losing focus, or are stressed, they can easily slip into your energy.

When I meditate, geometrical shapes always appear. My hand wants to draw these automatically. Why?

Because creation has come about through these primary patterns, basic patterns. When you are in a meditative state, your body gets in contact with these through your Higher Self. Use these patterns; they can strengthen you in your contact. New patterns will emerge gradually. The energy that comes to Earth includes the sacred geometric patterns.

How do I create my own reality and future?

In Pyramid 3 you find the frequencies for this. It is no coincidence that you are here right now. You have already made up your mind about your future. Past, present, and future can be compared to three sheets of paper that you can run a needle through. Everything exists at the same time. You can walk through these sheets simultaneously.

I just want to cry. Why?

Crying is a good tool that you have brought along. Just cry, and release the energies. For many people, crying is not enough, as their weight and burden is too heavy.

Which degrees of initiation do we have in this room?

When you talk about initiation, do you mean different levels of consciousness?

Yes.

You are on different levels with different knowledge (depending on earlier experiences), but all are ready for ascension or the inner transformation. Then it does not matter what experiences you brought with you, as long as you are ready to receive and raise your frequency. The day you ascend, you will not be visible to souls on a lower frequency level. You all have different vibrations, but we work with each one of you to help you rise in frequency. If you work with your blockages, it will be easier to be raised in frequency.

Thank you very much!
You are welcome, my friend; what do you thank me for?

I had an extremely strong feeling right after Christmas, when I contacted Thoth and felt such an incredibly strong presence. It was extremely meaningful for me.
You know that you can call upon me anytime you want, don't you? You have also, just like me, the ability to divide yourself on many planes at the same time. Remember, my friend, that from now on it is never again "I" but "We" in all your thoughts and in all your situations. You have to let go of your ego and take command over your life. The only one who can make a change is you, not I or anyone else.

I experience a nausea that comes and goes. Does it have to do with frequencies?
There are many who have felt this during the last period. Also, the body I am in. It has been going on for a few weeks, and it is a reaction to the raisings in frequency. One may have palpitations or nausea, a reaction that happens in your physical body. You know that you will change right down to the DNA level. Of course, changes happen slowly, a little every day.

So there is a fear at the bottom of this?
Your nausea is not fear that you carry right now, but a physical symptom of changes that are happening in your body.

Two weeks ago, I did an in depth journey. I met a person and had the experience of an explosion coming from inside, between the heart and the throat, and since then I have a problem with my heart, that it "jumps." What is going on?
One always opens the heart from the inside out. I have spoken

earlier about how you, when doing healing work, should take in the light from the back, straight through your heart. Imagine that you step out of your body so that you stand in front of yourself. Then step back into the body through the swinging doors that are opened inwards to the heart. Without my help, you are prepared for what is to come, so there is nothing strange, and you will continue to sense your heart for a time, because you have strong blockages located in this region, particularly from the age of three or early childhood years. It is about the family situation. Do you know what I am talking about? It is about to be released and disengaged, that is why you sense your heart. Your heart must be opened to the higher information.

Can I trust what I felt for the person I met and give in to this energy? It feels like I went into a deep trance, and I do not remember that much of the communication, but I feel that it is urgent.

If you recognize the man that you met today, then you can trust it! I have picked the best co-workers at each place. It is not easy to guard a pyramid where evil occurs daily (Pyramid 2). I do not mean spiritual evil, but that which happens on Earth in these regions: conflicts. I and everybody on my side think that the worst thing is that the conflicts happen in the name of a Higher Self. One allows oneself to use weapons in the name of Prime Creator, whether you call it God, Allah, or whatever it might be. Remember that you are all God, an aspect of God. Therefore, God does not exist on a higher plane, but you are God, each of you.

This area of conflict will be changed when key number two is opened. Before this era is over, changes will have happened there. Even though there are many who suffer in these regions, you shall all be aware that you yourself choose your life, your parents, and the place where you are going to live. If you have chosen a greater suffering, it means that you have chosen this life, and the purpose that this suffering is to achieve. Nothing is a coincidence.

Concluding Words from Paula

You have now taken note of Thoth's loving message to humanity. I hope that you, just like me, feel what a wonderful energy Thoth is, and I hope that his messages have given you new insights about the illusion of life and how everything is connected.

In a lecture in October 2011, Thoth spoke for the first time about the Matrix with the twelve etheric pyramids. On that occasion, he wanted us to search the internet for more information, as this was already written down. I found information about the pyramids on www.crystalinkinks.com. Unfortunately, I never found the source of these texts. With the approval of Thoth, I have used certain sentences from these texts to clarify the Matrix for you.

I also want to take the opportunity in these concluding words to thank everyone who helped me with this book. I want to give a big thank you to my best friend, Katarina Kaino, for all the wonderful, deep conversations, your commitment to proofread the texts, and for the fantastic and creative pictures that you created for this book. Thank you! Hans Björnell, I thank you also for all the help with proofreading. I also want to thank Eva Söder and Åsa for helping me to transcribe the texts from the recorded material, and many thanks to Maggan Karls for your financial support that helped me print the book. Finally, I also want to thank my wonderful husband and my three adorable children for bearing with me during the writing of this book.

A big hug to all of you!

Paula Rabenius

www.ingramcontent.com/pod-product-compliance
Lightning Source LLC
Chambersburg PA
CBHW071730120626
46550CB00002B/454